1982

THE *Joys* OF

RESEARCH

Walter Shropshire, Jr.   Editor

Smithsonian Institution Press
Washington, D.C., 1981

Library of Congress Cataloging in Publication Data
Main entry under title:
The Joys of research.
Talks presented at a colloquium celebrating the centennial
of the birth of Albert Einstein, held Mar. 16–17, 1979
at the Smithsonian Institution, Washington, D.C.
Includes bibliographical references and index.
Contents: Einstein and research/Paul Forman—
Biochemical pharmacology/Julius Axelrod—Mathematics/
I.M. Singer—[etc.]
1. Research—Congresses. 2. Science—Congresses.
3. Einstein, Albert, 1879–1955—Anniversaries, etc.
I. Shropshire, Walter. II. Einstein, Albert, 1879–1955.
III. Smithsonian Institution.
Q179.9.J69   001.4   81-9347
ISBN 0-87474-858-5   AACR2
ISBN 0-87474-857-7 (pbk.)

Frontispiece: A chortling Einstein is shown as he was lionized at Princeton in 1953.
[© 1979 by Ruth Orkin]

Dedication

In the Einstein Centennial Year the whole world joined in celebrating two things. Most obvious was the first: the intellectual achievement of a great mind seeking understanding of the material world. Less obvious but perhaps equally important was the second: the spirit and quality of the human being. Through no conscious effort on his part, people recognized in Albert Einstein a strain of decency and of idealism. In Einstein's mind that strain was part and parcel of his lifelong intellectual quest. It is to that spirit, that linkage of truth and decency, that the Smithsonian Institution dedicates this book.

S. DILLON RIPLEY
Secretary
The Smithsonian Institution

The Smithsonian Institution gratefully acknowledges contributions
in support of the colloquium from:
BASF Wyandotte Corporation
Bunker Ramo Corporation
Texas Instruments, Incorporated
and the United States Department of Energy

This publication was prepared with the support of Department of Energy
Grant No. DE-FG01-79ER-10042. Any opinions, findings, conclusions, or
recommendations are those of the authors and do not necessarily reflect
the views of the Department of Energy.

Contents

Michael Collins   Foreword   8

Walter Shropshire, Jr.   Preface   9

Paul Forman   INTRODUCTION: EINSTEIN AND RESEARCH   13

Julius Axelrod   BIOCHEMICAL PHARMACOLOGY   25

I. M. Singer   MATHEMATICS   38

Anna J. Harrison, Moderator   Axelrod-Singer Discussion   47

Howard M. Temin   ONCOLOGY AND VIROLOGY   58

George B. Field   THEORETICAL ASTROPHYSICS   65

André E. Hellegers, Moderator   Temin-Field Discussion   79

William Schuman   "ON FIRST HEARING": THE ACT OF CREATION IN MUSIC   page 86

Rosalyn S. Yalow   BIOMEDICAL INVESTIGATION   101

J. Tuzo Wilson   GEOPHYSICS   116

James D. Ebert, Moderator   Yalow-Wilson Discussion   126

Linus Pauling   CHEMISTRY   132

Ernst Mayr   EVOLUTIONARY BIOLOGY   147

William D. Carey, Moderator   Pauling-Mayr Discussion   158

Notes   163

Index   173

Foreword

The Smithsonian was honored by the presence of a group of distinguished speakers and listeners in a colloquium celebrating the centennial of the birth of Albert Einstein, one of the greatest figures in the history of science. In designing this event, the program committee decided neither to recount Einstein's achievements, nor to reassess them. Rather, it was decided the occasion called for a celebration of the spirit of the man, his extraordinary passion to comprehend the nature of the material world in order to fashion a theoretical explanation of the most general applicability. This extraordinary passion is expressed under the rubric, "The Joy of Research."

The Smithsonian's connection to Albert Einstein is indirect, but nonetheless quite real. We exist according to James Smithson's instructions for "the increase and diffusion of knowledge," and since 1846 the Institution has believed in research as an intellectual obligation and necessity. Research is a noble way of life. We are one of the few places in the United States with such a long, continuous tradition of supporting and conducting investigations in the physical, biological, and social sciences. We are proud that research has always been an honored word here at the Smithsonian.

Whatever drives scientists to observe, experiment, or calculate is rarely apparent in the finished product. For many generations, the published output of science has had an impersonal quality, perhaps to enhance the hope for objectivity of the results. But, for this impersonality, we have paid a price. The public at large does not realize the vital human nature of the scientific enterprise. What is sometimes seen as dry data or narrowly utilitarian facts may have originated from a sense of wonder or of beauty. The Einstein colloquium, we hope, demonstrated these very human motivations and responses in research. We asked the speakers to talk directly of their own experiences and thereby stimulate the rest of us to reflect and to ask questions of them and of ourselves. From their remarks, we may begin to understand why science has attracted such a devoted body of men and women to what is clearly one of the greatest joys and achievements of humanity.

MICHAEL COLLINS
Former Undersecretary
of the Smithsonian Institution

Preface

Throughout the world, the life and accomplishments of Albert Einstein were celebrated during the centennial of his birth. As part of this celebration in the United States, the Smithsonian Institution invited eight renowned scientists to participate in a small colloquium held at the Carmichael Auditorium of the National Museum of American History on March 16 and 17, 1979. The audience consisted of young students entering or contemplating entry into research careers, scientists actively pursuing current problems, and accomplished researchers who had moved to positions of administering scientific research.

The scientists were invited to share their autobiographies, with a special emphasis upon the factors and circumstances that drew them into research careers. Because the organizing committee for this colloquium recognized that there would be many celebrations reviewing the scientific achievements of Einstein, the decision was made to celebrate instead the enthusiasm and excitement that scientists share for research. Einstein himself expressed this eloquently in an interview with William Miller for *Life* magazine in 1955:

> The important thing is not to stop questioning. Curiosity has its own reason for existence. One cannot help but be in awe when he contemplates the mysteries of eternity, of life, of the marvelous structure of reality. It is enough if one tries merely to comprehend a little of this mystery each day. Never lose a holy curiosity.

Einstein also enjoyed music. Therefore, the organizing committee felt that a concert would make a welcome and refreshing interlude in the colloquium. It would also give an opportunity to explore some of the similarities between creativity in the arts and sciences. On Friday evening, March 16, the colloquium moved to the auditorium of the National Academy of Sciences, and with an enlarged audience from the scientific and musical communities of Washington, D.C., enjoyed an extraordinary concert.

Following a performance of Bach's suite no. 1 in G Major by violist Donald McInnes, the audience was treated to the Washington première of a new composition by the American composer William Schuman, who introduced his work "In Sweet Music," a serenade on a setting of Shakespeare for flute, viola, voice, and harp, by describing how he came to compose it.

At the conclusion of the performance, the Jubal Trio and Lucy Shelton, soprano, were joined on stage by William Schuman. An open exchange of ideas flowed between the audience, the performers, and the composer as comments and questions were shared about the joys of creativity in musical composition and performance.

Because of the richness of exchange between speakers and participants, a decision was made to prepare this book. The organizing committee felt that since the audience was a relatively small, invited one, it would be desirable to have a wider distribution of the content of this celebration.

The chapters that follow were prepared by transcribing tape recordings of the individual presentations. They were extensively edited, and then corrected by the speakers themselves. Great effort was expended, however, to preserve some of the spontaneous enthusiasm evidenced, particularly in the discussion following the paired talks. To set the stage for the volume, an Introduction by Paul Forman has been added. He gives some insights into the motivating forces that led the young Einstein into a research career.

The subsequent material may be read at several levels. For the scientist, trained professionally in the same subject matter as the speaker, there are details of interest only to the specialist. Interwoven with these abstruse facts is rich material of interest to biographers, sociologists, and students, searching for encouragement to enter science as a research career. It is my belief that even a very general reader, unskilled in science, will be able to recognize clearly both the motivating and the frustrating factors encountered by these successful scientists as they have pursued their research.

I wish to thank and acknowledge the support and assistance of a number of persons in making the completion of this volume possible. They are: Audrey Shropshire, my wife, who supported and encouraged the entire work; Joan HajShafi, who transcribed the original tapes; the office staff of the Smithsonian Radiation Biology Laboratory, Carolyn Walker, Joan HajShafi, Karen Applestein, and Leslie Spurlock, for typing and indexing skills; Angela Haggins and Mary Clare Gray for library assistance; the staff of the Office of Smithsonian Symposia and Seminars, Wilton S. Dillon, director, Barrick W. Groom, Dorothy Richardson, and especially Carla M. Borden, associate director, who prepared the printed program for the colloquium and the biographical sketches of the speakers; Elizabeth A. Sur and Hope Pantell of the Smithsonian Institution Press for design and editorial assistance respectively; the Smithsonian Institution program committee for the colloquium, chaired by Nathan Reingold, for organizing and selecting the list of speakers and participants; and finally, Lou Chatfield, Max Delbrück, Robert Dumm, James R. Morgan, Roy D. Morrison II, and Tom Roman, friends who gave much encouragement and many helpful suggestions.

WALTER SHROPSHIRE, JR.
Rockville, Maryland

Figure 1. Albert at perhaps four years of age.

Figure 2. Albert, about six, with his sister, Maja.

Introduction: Einstein and Research

PAUL FORMAN
Curator of Modern Physics, National Museum of American History

Before the undersigned official there appeared today the, personally known, merchant Hermann Einstein, resident in Ulm, Bahnhofstrasse B. Nr 135, of israelite religion, and announced that to Pauline Einstein, née Koch, his wife by marriage, of israelite religion, resident with him in Ulm in his residence, on the fourteenth of March of the year one thousand eight hundred seventy nine in the morning about half past eleven o'clock a child of male sex was born, which received the given name Albert.[1]

Thus the birth of Albert Einstein was recorded by the municipal clerk of Ulm in the province of Swabia, where Einstein's German-Jewish forebears had lived since the eighteenth century. Albert's only sibling, Marie (Maja), with whom he had a close relationship and who was very similar to her brother in appearance as well as character, was born two years later in Munich. There their father had joined his younger brother, Jacob, an electrical engineer, in operating J. Einstein & Co., a firm for the manufacture of electrical equipment and the installation of muncipal electric-lighting systems. (Their electrifications included Schwabing, soon to become Munich's artistic quarter, and some small northern Italian towns.)[2] Whatever Hermann's deficiencies as a businessman—and in time they became distressingly evident—he was, by all indications, an affectionate, tolerant father. Albert was fond of him, and his death in 1902, though long expected, was a severe shock.

From the time Albert was six until the middle of his sixteenth year, the two families shared a large house adjacent to their factory, some hundreds of feet back from the road on a well-treed lot in the suburbs of Munich. Here "they led a rather retired life," one of their few regular guests recalled, "mingling little with neighbors or other people."[3] Albert was a quiet and rather shy child. He did not begin to talk before three years of age—because, he is reported to have recalled, he had very early conceived the ambition of speaking in complete sentences.[4] Even at age nine, in the

Figure 3. Hermann Einstein, Albert's father.

Figure 4. Pauline Koch Einstein, Albert's mother.

last class of elementary school, his speech was halting, partly because of the further condition he imposed upon his utterances, namely, perfect honesty and accuracy. Among his classmates he gained the nickname *Biedermeier* ("straight arrow").

In these early years, religion came to play an important role in Einstein's conception of the meaning of his existence. Although his parents, following the common path of emancipation and assimilation, had ceased to observe Jewish rites and possibly deprecated religious beliefs, they nonetheless saw to it that their son received private tuition in Judaism. This was the more necessary, they perhaps felt, because, for convenience's sake, they sent Albert to the local elementary school, a Roman Catholic institution. There, as the only Jew in his class, he participated in Catholic religious lessons. "Physical assaults and insults were frequent on the way to school," Einstein recalled; "they were enough to confirm, even in a child of my age, a vivid feeling of not belonging."[5]

The ambiguity of this situation was intolerable to the young Einstein. His response was a "deep religiosity,"[6]—including the composition and singing of hymns, abstinence from pork, and other behavior quite in opposition to the general tenor of his elders' household. This orientation was probably strengthened and supported when, at age ten, he entered the *Gymnasium* (high school), for here religious instruction was given the

Figure 5. Albert at about age fourteen.

Figure 6. Albert, about fourteen, with his sister, Maja.

Jewish students by an able and sensitive rabbi, whose teachings made a strong impression upon the youth. (Einstein's later recollections notwithstanding, the *Gymnasium* he attended in Munich was a relatively new and progressive institution, where liberal ideas and ideals were not unknown, and where Einstein had at least a few teachers whom he esteemed.)

This religious phase ended, abruptly, when Einstein was about twelve. The emphatic swing into disbelief was precipitated by the reading of popular books on natural science to which Albert was introduced by an indigent medical student, who, following the traditional forms of Jewish charity, came once a week to dine with the Einsteins. Persuaded by this scientistic literature, and doubtless also by much that he heard discussed at home, that the Bible was untrue, and conceiving that in religious instruction youth was being deliberately deceived, the young Albert entered a new phase of "fanatical freethinking," as he later described it.[7] Far from being left a cynic, however, Einstein found in mathematics and natural science, especially as presented by nineteenth-century scientistic writers, an alternative world view and means of escape from "the merely pesonal."[8]

This conversion was based, to be sure, upon Einstein's own natural gifts and inclinations, but also upon earlier experiences whose latent force only now emerged. The strongest of these, one which Einstein frequently recalled and underscored in later years, was the impression produced upon him by the uncanny behavior of a magnetic compass. This was shown him by his father in an effort to amuse the four- or five-year-old when sick abed with one of many childhood ailments. What seized Einstein and determined, as it seemed to him, the direction of his thought and life was the contradiction it presented to his already well-developed sense of physical causation.

It is perhaps more than coincidence that Einstein's earliest known essay in science,[9] a manuscript of a half-dozen pages written at age sixteen, is a sketch of a research program to determine "the state of the aether in a magnetic field," i.e., the physical mechanism by which the behavior of a compass needle is controlled. Perhaps also Einstein's unremitting preoccupation with causality, his insistence upon it and upon grasping it, may be connected with this powerful early experience. Moreover, the character of the business enterprise carried on in the building next door, and the daily contact with his uncle the engineer—whose playful introduction of the youth to algebra was also long remembered—probably helped awaken Einstein's scientific interest.

The autumn of 1894 saw the abandonment of the Einsteins' retreat in suburban Sendlingen. Albert was left as a roomer in Munich to continue his schooling, while his parents and sister moved to Milan in search of better business opportunities. Unhappy at the separation from his family and at the prospect of spending three lonely years completing the *Gymnasium*, Albert, at the cost of a bad conscience, persuaded a friendly doctor to write a medical excuse for absenting him from school, secured from his mathematics teacher a testimonial to his exceptional knowledge, and early in 1895 joined his family in sunny Italy.

In this delightful environment, with no school to attend, Albert had perfect freedom to pursue his own intellectual interests. It was there in the spring or summer of 1895 that the young man drafted the program mentioned above for determining experimentally "the elastic deformations" of the aether in a magnetic field "together with the cause bringing them about."[10] Although containing serious weaknesses and confusions, the paper is most impressively mature in language and mode of expression, and especially in the grasp it displays of the strategy and goals of physical research.

Even before his family departed for Milan, Albert had begged his father to allow him to renounce his German nationality. Perhaps he already foresaw the terrible situation in which he would be placed by withdrawal from his *Gymnasium*. The universal military service law of the German Empire imposed quite disparate obligations upon those who had completed their studies at a German secondary school (who had had the *Abitur*) and those who had not attained this educational qualification. In the former case, just one year of service was required—and that under very mild conditions in the company of other "academics"; in the latter case, three years under very rough conditions. Einstein's solution to this problem was simple but radical: renunciation of German citizenship. Shortly before the statutory deadline—the prospective recruit's seventeenth birthday—Einstein's father submitted the necessary petition in his son's name. For the next five years Einstein was stateless. His goal, Swiss citizenship, was gained in 1901, the year following his graduation from the Zurich Polytechnic.

Admission to this elite institution—the only German-language institution of university caliber to which entrance could be gained by examination—had presumably already been part of Einstein's plan in leaving Munich. Early in the autumn of 1895 Einstein, still two or three years below the usual age of entrance, presented himself in Zurich for examination. His knowledge of mathematics and physics was judged exceptional, but of history and foreign languages unacceptable. At the recommendation of one of his examiners, Einstein spent a year at the secondary school of the neighboring canton of Aargau.

Einstein boarded in the commune of Aarau with one of his instructors at the *Kantonschule*, Jost Winteler, a pioneer in the analysis of German dialects, whose leading generalization was the concept of linguistic "relativity."[11] Thoroughly adopted by this warm and intellectual family, Einstein addressed Mrs. Winteler as "Mamerl," little mama. Einstein's sister followed him to Aarau, frequented the Wintelers' home for several years while studying there, and eventually married the Wintelers' son.

It was probably at this time that Einstein resolved upon a life in science. When he first set sights upon the Zurich Polytechnic, he, or at least his elders, had a career in engineering in view. In later years Einstein was intrigued by technical processes, devices, and gadgets of every sort, and it is unlikely that this fascination was entirely owing to his later employment as a patent examiner. Rather, it must have been evident in his childhood as well. But while attracted intellectually, Einstein was repelled morally—by the social consequences and mercenary goal of the engineers' activity. By the time Einstein left Aarau, where he was exposed to an outstanding instructor in physics and had access to a truly exceptional physics laboratory,[12] he had made up his mind to enroll in the polytechnic's pure science curriculum, which was intended to prepare secondary-school teachers of physics and mathematics.

In a brief French essay, written in September 1896 as his school-leaving examination in that subject, Einstein described "My plans for the future":

> If I have the good fortune to pass my examinations successfully, I shall go to the Federal Institute of Technology in Zurich. I shall stay there four years in order to study mathematics and physics. I imagine myself becoming a professor in those branches of the natural sciences, choosing the theoretical parts of them.
>
> Here are the causes that have brought me to this plan. Above all is the

Figure 7. Albert at age seventeen, upon graduation from high school in Aarau, Switzerland.

individual disposition for abstract and mathematical thought, the lack of fantasy and of practical talent. There are also my desires, which had led me to the same resolve. This is quite natural. One always likes to do those things for which one has talent. Besides, there is also a certain independence in the scientific profession that greatly pleases me.[13]

Two words are especially to be noted in this quotation: "causes" in the first sentence of the second paragraph and "independence" in the last. The first of these key words (rightly changed to "reasons" by the corrector of Einstein's examination paper) is our earliest example of Einstein's adherence to causality in a more general sense, a conviction that every phenomenon—not merely physical or biological, but also behavioral or volitional—is completely determined.[14] The second, the *Unabhängigkeitsdrang*, the pressing need for independence, was the characteristic by which those who knew Einstein as a young man were most impressed—either favorably or unfavorably.

By virtue of this characteristic, Einstein was never and nowhere more than a mediocre student; not at his German secondary school, where he was unhappy, nor at his Swiss, where he was very happy. Not even at the Polytechnic could he bring himself to jump through hoops, though most of his teachers were excellent scientists, on the one hand, and, on the other hand, he was acutely aware of the precariousness of his family's circumstances and thus of the necessity for him to look to his future. Of his career at the "Poly," Einstein recalled at the very end of his life:

> I soon saw that I had to content myself with being a mediocre student. In order to be a good student one must have an effortlessness in comprehension; willingness to concentrate all one's powers upon the assigned material; love of order, so that one makes notes on the lectures and afterwards conscientiously works them out. All these qualities I lacked entirely—as I regretfully recognized. Thus I gradually learned, with something of a guilty conscience, to live quietly by myself and arrange my studies so as to agree with my intellectual stomach and my interests. A few lectures I followed with intense interest. Otherwise, however, I "cut" a lot and studied at home with holy zeal . . . the masters of theoretical physics. A fellow student from Serbia [Yugoslavia], Mileva Maric, whom I later married, participated in these private studies. [15]

Little wonder, then, that while each of the other three students in his section graduating in 1900 received appointments to assistantships at the Polytechnic and therewith the opportunity for further education and a start in the academic world, Einstein received no support or encouragement from his teachers. His principal instructor in physics, H. F. Weber, remarked to him at the time, "You're a clever boy, Einstein, a very clever boy. But you have one great fault: you won't let anyone tell you anything!"[16] And his principal instructor in mathematics, Hermann Minkowski, remarked of him eight or nine years later, after he had become well known through the theory of relativity, "I wouldn't have thought Einstein capable of that; in Zurich he knew nothing."[17]

For two difficult years Einstein lived from hand to mouth, on a series of temporary jobs, while seeking in every direction for a foothold in the academic world. Finally, early in the summer of 1902 Einstein accepted a position as an examiner in the Swiss Patent Office, where he was obliged to be at his desk eight hours a day, six days a week. This was no academic job, but the security thus obtained made possible his marriage to Mileva, and by the summer of 1904 Einstein was learning to shut out even the sounds of a crying child as he concentrated in the evenings upon his scientific investigations.

In view of the novelty and the importance of the ideas which Einstein thus evolved in his leisure hours, it would be easy—and it certainly is common—

Figure 8. Einstein at his desk in the Swiss Patent Office, 1908.

to describe Einstein as a revolutionary in science. Yet a revolutionary guise seems improbable for one who, like Einstein, was personally committed to the scientific enterprise while isolated socially and intellectually from his fellow physicists. In fact, while his academic colleagues were behaving like self-conscious revolutionaries—striving to replace the mechanistic world picture with one founded upon Maxwell's electromagnetic-field theory and the newly discovered electron—Einstein sustained himself with the notion that he was in the best tradition of theoretical physics, extending and completing the program of reduction of the science to the mechanics of particles.[18] It was this program which underlay all of Einstein's highly original and seemingly diverse proposals of 1905: light quanta, Brownian motion, and "an electrodynamics of moving bodies, based upon a modification of the doctrine of space and time."[19]

Throughout his life Einstein remained unsympathetic to the notion of scientific revolutions and to physicists who saw their work in such terms.[20] True, Einstein himself, in his later years, appeared a rebel in his dress, opinion, and behavior. Yet his disregard of the conventions of social life carried so little of the demonstrativeness, the *pointe*, that accompanies rebellious intent, that the word "rebel" or "revolutionary" seems quite inappropriate. Indeed it would be truer to say that it was precisely because Einstein was, in his own mind, so far from being a rebel in his scientific work and goals, so fully and surely part of an intellectual enterprise transcending time and place, that he could so easily, so lightly disregard conventions of everyday life which he found constraining.

Einstein remained in Berne, at the Patent Office, for seven intensely creative and productive years. He wrote papers and sent them off for publication to the leading German-language physics journal, *Annalen der Physik*, but he made no effort to come into personal contact with his academic colleagues. The breed was not, he had decided, at all congenial to him and, as he vaguely recognized, their scientific orientation was the opposite of his own. Inevitably, however, after 1905, scientific recognition—and even visits by academic colleagues—gradually came to Einstein at the Patent Office. In the autumn of 1909 he left that "secular cloister where I had my best ideas" for his first scientific congress and his first academic post. Einstein changed jobs thrice again within four years, arriving in the spring of 1914 at the apex of the academic world, a research professorship at the Prussian Academy of Sciences in Berlin.

What then were the "joys of research" for Einstein? We must expect and accept that the personal satisfactions, the "kicks" which Einstein derived from his work, are of a rather different nature than those of the average scientist, or even than those of most of the best scientists. This is evident merely from the fact of Einstein's early researches having been carried out in such perfect freedom, i.e., without any material or social incentives or constraints. For without such inducements, intensive, sustained intellectual activity is rare indeed, be it in science or in any other field of human endeavor outside the arts.

It was only gradually, painfully, in the years following his graduation from the Polytechnic, that Einstein had given up the idea of an academic career. Yet once reconciled to being an avocational investigator, Einstein recognized the genuine advantages inherent in the circumstance, and afterward repeatedly emphasized that a situation in which one is paid to produce research is ipso facto demoraliziing. Although he himself remained ever ready to accept this burden in exchange for greater leisure to pursue his thoughts, Einstein never ceased to believe that

> Science is a wonderful thing if one does not have to earn one's living at it. One should earn one's living by work of which one is sure one is capable. Only when we do not have to be accountable to anybody can we find joy in scientific endeavour. [21]

Not that joy per se was, in Einstein's view, sufficient either as motivation or justification for scientific endeavor. Suppose, said Einstein—he was thirty-nine and this was the first time he had addressed such questions in public—an angel of the Lord were to drive from the temple of science not merely those scientists "who make their sacrificial offering of brain grease only for the sake of utilitarian ends," but also the far commoner and not wholly inestimable sort who "occupies himself with science in the joyful feeling of superior intellectual power," for whom "science is his proper sport, and brings him forceful experiences and satisfaction of his ambition." All these banished, who would then remain in the temple of science? Few, a precious few, said Einstein. [22]

While Einstein did not wish to give a single, uniform answer to the question of what led those few into scientific pursuits, he stressed that it was less the activity per se than the *goal* of the activity: the desire "to form a simplified, synoptic picture of the world" was of first importance to these "somewhat peculiar, reserved, solitary fellows." Neither did Einstein push his metaphor so hard as to speak here of holy men devoted to understanding how God ordained His word. Yet clearly his thoughts were pointing in that direction. In the succeeding decades of his life Einstein spoke ever more often and directly in such terms, and came to regard himself as "a man possessed. As in my youth, I sit here endlessly and think and calculate, hoping to unearth deep secrets." [23]

A good example of this perseverance, this tenacity, and, above all, this thorough independence in the pursuit of understanding, is Einstein's achievement of the theory of relativity. The negative results of the Michelson-Morley experiment designed to reveal the motion of the earth relative to the ether, although one of the main difficulties leading his contemporaries toward similar conceptions, was not even mentioned in Einstein's first papers on relativity and was probably of little importance in the development of his ideas. [24] Rather, the paradox which had moved and focused his thoughts from the time he was still a pupil in Aarau revolved around this question: how would a light wave appear when viewed by an observer moving in the same direction at the same speed? The obvious answer was that it should appear as static electric and magnetic fields whose magnitudes oscillated sinusoidally in space. "There does not, however, appear to be any such thing," Einstein said, "neither on the basis of experience nor according to Maxwell's equations. From the very beginning it appeared to me intuitively clear that, judged from the standpoint of such an observer everything would have to happen according to the same laws as for an observer at rest relative to the earth." [25] After ten years of puzzling over this problem, uniquely *his* problem, it occurred to Einstein in the spring of 1905 that "time was suspect." From the moment of that insight to the completion of a paper—*the* paper—was then just a matter of weeks.

We have no record of what Einstein felt in those bright Bernese spring days of 1905, but perhaps there was some similarity to his feelings in those dark Berlin winter days in December 1915 during which he completed the general theory of relativity, after another ten years of far more intense searching, groping, yearning. "Imagine my joy," he wrote his friend Paul Ehrenfest, "at the feasibility of general covariance [of the equations for the gravitational field] and at the result that the equations yield the correct motion of mercury's perihelion! For several days I was beside myself with joyful excitement."[26] Which of us has experienced joy of such intensity? Perhaps as a result of attaining a long-coveted prize, perhaps a wife, perhaps a job. But as a result of attaining the object of our intellectual labors!

Of course, such joy was experienced by Einstein but few times in his life. Between these isolated pinnacles there were many lower peaks and high plateaus. As he wrote to his fellow student and faithful friend, Marcel Grossman, while in the midst of his first theoretical research, "It is a wonderful feeling to recognize the unity of a complex of phenomena which, perceived directly by our senses, seem to be entirely separate things."[27] Nor was the pleasure of mental exercise for its own sake unknown to Einstein. "When I have no special problem to occupy my mind, I love to reconstruct proofs of mathematical and physical theorems that have long been known to me. There is no *goal* in this, merely an opportunity to indulge in the pleasant occupation of thinking."[28] Yet between this "pleasant occupation of thinking" and the stubborn assault upon a salient of physical reality there was an enormous difference, not merely of degree but of kind. The latter endeavor, the striving "to trace *His* lines after Him," is a Promethean undertaking, and, as such, carried with it the peculiar thrill of hubris.[29]

This goal, to know *His* thoughts, and the joyful excitement at its attainment, were expressions of Einstein's wish "to flee from everyday life with its painful roughness and hopeless dreariness, to flee from the chains of one's own ever-changing desires."[30] "It is quite clear to me," Einstein wrote late in life, "that the religious paradise of my youth which I lost was a first attempt to free myself from the chains of the 'merely personal,' from the existence which is dominated by wishes, hopes and primitive feelings."[31] This intent, and devotion to theoretical natural science as the means for attaining it, were firmly fixed in Einstein by the time he had reached late adolescence. "Strenuous intellectual effort and the contemplation of God's creation are the angels which will guide me, reconciling, strengthening, and yet with uncompromising rigor, through all the disquiets and conflicts of this life."[32]

It might thus appear that Einstein was quite indifferent to, or at least derived no real pleasure from, recognition of his accomplishments by his fellow scientists. In one sense this was true. Yet at the same time, "passionate striving" after truth not merely "frees us from the bonds of the 'I,' " but also "makes us comrades of those who are the best and the greatest."[33] Einstein placed a high value upon his participation in this select fraternity. Is this not, he asked, shaking his head at the chauvinism of scientists during the First World War, "the only 'Fatherland' which men of our type can take seriously?"[34] And again, bitterly depressed in the midst of the Second World War, he felt that "in the timeless community of people of this sort one finds a sort of refuge that fends off desperation and feelings of hopeless isolation."[35]

Just because the joys Einstein derived from his research were, when they came, so genuine, he had no need to bolster himself for this extraordinarily arduous activity with romantic illusions about intellectual work. "Whoever knows it does not go tearing after it," his colleague Arnold Sommerfeld recalled him saying early on. This same view Einstein expressed again, simply and engagingly, in a quatrain he wrote toward the end of his life:

> In thought to be absorbed, to strain
> and to overtax the brain,
> Not everyone will undertake
> if at all he can escape.[36]

The implication is that for Einstein there is no escape, that *he* is condemned to this ceaseless straining of the brain: "All year long the Sphinx stares at me in reproach and reminds me painfully of the uncomprehended, blotting out the personal aspects of life."[37] And indeed, what originally was his choice, became his fate. He is "a man possessed," "fanatical";[38] "I do the thing which my own nature drives me to do."[39]

Biochemical Pharmacology

JULIUS AXELROD

Chief, Section on Pharmacology, Laboratory of Clinical Science, National Institute of Mental Health; editorial board of numerous scientific journals; member, National Academy of Sciences; winner of Nobel Prize for Physiology or Medicine, 1970.

"I wished to study medicine, but for financial and other reasons was unable to attend medical school. . . . In 1946, I obtained a position in the laboratory of Dr. Bernard B. Brodie at Goldwater Memorial Hospital, New York University. It was in this stimulating atmosphere that I [acquired] my initial experience as an investigator. During this period, in collaboration with Dr. Brodie, I developed methods for and described the metabolic fate of several analgesic and anticoagulant drugs in man. . . .

"My major fields of research interest are biochemical mechanisms of drug and hormone actions, drug and hormone metabolism, enzymology and the pineal gland. . . . At present, I am involved in studying the role of phospholipids in membrane structure and function and in the metabolism of estrogens in the brain."

Successful scientists generally are recognized early. They go to the best schools, train under the very best people, publish early, and are recognized. None of this happened to me.

I was born in a ghetto on the Lower East Side of New York, and I wanted to become a doctor. I attended public schools and City College in New York, a free tuition school that provided me a wonderful opportunity to get an education. In those days, it was extremely difficult for a graduate of City College to get into a medical school, but I had a choice. It was 1933 and in the depths of the depression. I passed an examination for post office clerk with a very nice salary. I also heard of a position as a laboratory worker for William H. Park, a noted bacteriologist at NYU Medical School. The position paid twenty-five dollars a month and I made the fateful decision to work in a laboratory, rather than at the post office at forty dollars a week.

I enjoyed working as an assistant to Dr. K. G. Falk, who was head of the laboratory, until it became difficult financially for me. I wanted to get married, so I got a position in a food-testing laboratory, where I worked for ten years. It wasn't a bad job; it involved the development of methods. I learned it was extremely important to any kind of research to develop your own methods.

One day the laboratory got a contract from a group of manufacturers of headache powders who had problems. They found that people who take, for example, Bromo Seltzer, got methemoglobinemia. [Methemoglobin of the blood causes dizziness, headaches, diarrhea, and anemia.] The manufacturers wanted to know why. My chief asked me if I would be willing to tackle this problem. I said, "Well, I never did any type of research of this kind." The chief said, "I know a bright biochemist, Dr. B. B. Brodie, who works at the Goldwater Memorial Hospital here in New York. He might help you."

I called Dr. Brodie and he said, "Why don't you come down and talk to me?" We sat and chatted. He asked, "What is the active principle in reducing headaches in these powders?" I said, "acetanilide." He answered, "You know if one takes any chemical into the body, it's transformed."

This one statement was a revelation to me and we started to think together. He said, "Put the chemical structure on the board. What kind of a compound could be transformed to a methemoglobin-forming compound? One possibly is aniline" [fig. 9].

Figure 9.

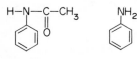

Acetanilide   Aniline

I think that one conversation did more for me than most any type of graduate study. *We learned to ask the right questions.* If aniline was the compound responsible for causing this blood disease, it should be found in the blood after headache powders are ingested. Of course, you would have to develop an extremely sensitive method to detect it in the blood. This was one thing I was good at—developing methods. I devised a method for aniline and sure enough, when we gave acetanilide, we found aniline in the blood. It also caused methemoglobinemia. For the crucial experiment, we gave aniline to dogs to see if methemoglobinemia occurred. It did! I took the aniline myself. I turned blue, but at least I proved a point! I became a great enthusiast for research.

This was a very fateful experience in my life. I learned how to do research. I found that it required first a tremendous dedication, devotion. You think about your problem all the time. It never leaves your mind. It isn't hard work that does it. It's a matter of thinking about the problem in new ways. The important thing is to ask a question that is realistic. Medawar says, "Research is the art of the soluble."[1]

Fortunately, Goldwater Memorial Hospital was just the right place to be because it was full of very bright young researchers. Goldwater, at the end of the Second World War, was assigned to work on developing new antimalarial drugs. The Japanese had cut off the supply of quinine during the war. In developing these antimalarial drugs, ideas were thrown about, one after another. Of course, ideas are worthless unless they're testable. But I had an opportunity to really become a scientist in that atmosphere in a short period. There were lots of spinoffs.

One of the spinoffs was that another compound was being formed in the body from acetanilide. We identified it as N-acetyl para-aminophenol [fig. 10]. I don't know whether you recognize this compound, but we suggested

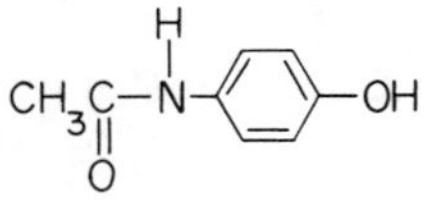

Figure 10. N-acetyl-para-aminophenol (acetaminophen) Tylenol®

that it should be used instead of acetanilide because it is an analgesic and it is less toxic.[2] This started a multimillion-dollar industry, Tylenol.® For this suggestion we received ten thousand dollars as a research grant to continue our work.

The thing about research is to know what to do next after you solve a problem. One thing leads to another. I might add that research isn't entirely joyous. You have to have an ability to tolerate lots of frustration and ambiguity. You have to know when to persist on a problem and when to give up because it might lead nowhere.

After working at Goldwater for three years, I realized there was no future for me. I didn't have a Ph.D. degree, and without a Ph.D., in an academic institution, you get nowhere no matter how good you are. I just didn't feel like getting a Ph.D. then. I was thirty-five and I liked doing research. I was married, with children. I just couldn't take the time off. About this time I heard of a position at the National Institutes of Health and decided to join them. This was another very wise move on my part. It was the right place to be.

I continued my work on the metabolism of drugs and was attracted by an unusual group of compounds called sympathomimetic amines. These are compounds described by the great pharmacologist Sir Henry Dale as "mimicking the actions of certain aspects of the nervous system, the sympathetic nervous system."[3] I picked one of these compounds to work on—amphetamine [fig. 11]. Amphetamine, which had been synthesized

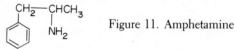

Figure 11. Amphetamine

a few years before, had very unusual properties. If one took lots of it, it was as though one had paranoid schizophrenia.

I was interested in what happened to this compound in the body, and I worked out its fate. In the course of this work, I had to become an enzymologist. I wanted to find out how the body can take care of so many foreign, strange compounds; even synthetic compounds, possibly thousands of them. How does the body recognize such a compound, which might be toxic? How does it get rid of this compound? In order to understand how the body did this, I began studying what enzymes are involved and their enzymatic mechanisms.

Enzymes are catalysts in the body that transform normally occurring compounds from one to another for the body's special purposes. Although I knew very little enzymology, there fortunately was a very bright young man, the late Gordon Tomkins, in my laboratory.[4] Tomkins, who became a well-known molecular biologist, said, "Julie, you know there's no big mystery being an enzymologist. All you have to have is a razor blade and a liver. Have you got a method for amphetamine?"

"Yes."

He said, "Why don't you throw amphetamine in a liver slice."

Sure enough, the amphetamine was metabolized. Within one month of asking the right question of the right person and trying not to think in orthodox ways, I found that the enzyme that metabolizes amphetamine was a very unusual one. Now, it's recognized as a very well-known class of enzymes, P_{450} enzymes. It does lots of things: metabolizes thousands of foreign compounds, may form carcinogens, and, its main role, detoxifies drugs. The enzyme also has a very unusual property: it requires not only oxygen but reduces pyridine nucleotides—and it was a complete mystery to me how this type of a reaction could be carried out. This is understood now, but the point is, such research doesn't require lots of training and a great mind. I think you just have to ask the right questions at the right time and you have to ask the right people for advice.

I wanted to get a promotion at NIH, but I didn't have a Ph.D. Although I had published forty papers and discovered these drug-metabolizing enzymes, an administrator said, "unless you have a Ph.D., you cannot get a promotion." So I decided to take my Ph.D. at George Washington University. Using my work on the drug-metabolizing enzymes as my thesis, I finally got the degree at age forty-two.[5]

I had worked at the National Heart Institute but wanted to try some new things, so I sent my application to the Cancer Institute and to the Institute on Mental Health. I was hired by Mental Health, and this opportunity again changed the course of my work.

When I joined the institute, I felt as most of us feel many times in a new field. There is a sense of insecurity. Therefore, I decided to work on problems similar to those I was used to, the metabolism of drugs. I selected the metabolism of morphine, which I felt was a bit more appropriate to the mission of the NIH. I also studied the metabolism of LSD and I became interested in a group of compounds of nerve chemicals called neurotransmitters as a result of my work on amphetamine.

Neurotransmitters are chemical signals that are released from the nerve and cause a specific response in cells. They have a very unusual history. The first concept was proposed about eighty years ago by a graduate student, T. R. Elliot, at Cambridge University. Elliot found that when he injected adrenaline, a compound that had been isolated from the adrenal gland just recently by John Abel at Johns Hopkins, it produced effects similar to that of stimulating the sympathetic nervous system.[6] Elliot proposed that nerves can liberate chemicals. His professor at Cambridge, J. N. Langley, a noted physiologist, was very cold to this suggestion and said, "Go and get some more facts and the theory will make itself."[7] Elliot proposed this idea in an abstract to the Physiology Society. In his larger paper, later, he didn't mention it at all.[8] He didn't want to antagonize his professor!

However, it was Otto Loewi, an Austrian pharmacologist, who believed in chemical neurotransmission. He sought the right experiment to prove it and one day he had a dream; he dreamt of the experiment to prove chemical nerve transmission. He woke up, scribbled down the experiment, went back to sleep, and when he got up the next morning he couldn't read his handwriting! Fortunately, he had the same dream again. This is a true story, recorded in his autobiography.[9] This time he immediately dashed to the laboratory and did the experiment. It was very elegant. He took two beating frog hearts, put them in a common bath, and stimulated the vagus nerve of

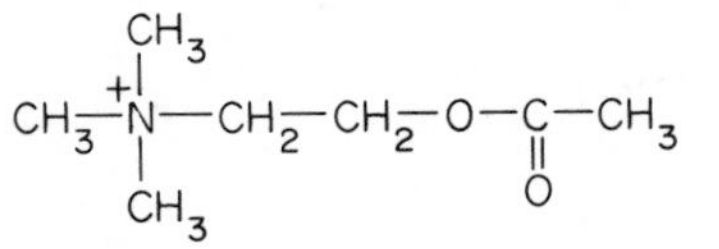

$$CH_3-\overset{\overset{\displaystyle CH_3}{|}}{\underset{\underset{\displaystyle CH_3}{|}}{\overset{+}{N}}}-CH_2-CH_2-O-\overset{\overset{\displaystyle }{}}{\underset{\underset{\displaystyle O}{\|}}{C}}-CH_3$$

Figure 12. Acetylcholine

one heart. This slowed the beat of the second heart, indicating that some chemical was liberated from the heart. This chemical was isolated and identified as acetylcholine [fig. 12].

Sometimes, this is how research is done. If your mind is too occupied with your experiments, you don't think. It is usually during a time of reverie or boredom that solutions to problems can be reached. It is while your mind wanders that you really think of the right experiment.

There are many such examples. The German chemist Kekulé, I think, was sitting on a bus and had a reverie. He thought of the right structure of the benzene ring.[10] I have had occasions like that many times; while listening to boring lectures I have thought of the right experiment. My mind wanders and I think of something that's bothering me about yesterday's experiment. Something clicks—not all the time but many times.

I still was very much interested in neurotransmitters. One day at a seminar, the head of my laboratory, Seymour Kety, a well-known neuroscientist, gave a fascinating report. He had visited two Canadian psychiatrists who claimed that when adrenaline is left out in the air, it turns pink. When you give this compound to a person, it causes hallucinations. They proposed that mental illness might be caused by an abnormal metabolism of adrenaline.

I was fascinated. This was a very imaginative type of hypothesis. Looking into the literature, I found that there was nothing known about what happens to adrenaline in the body. Aha! This was a great problem to work on because it might be directly related to the mission of the Institute on Mental Health. I'd also had some background in studying the metabolism of a related group of compounds, amphetamines. I began this problem and spent three frustrating months trying to find an oxidative pathway for adrenaline. I couldn't find it.

One day, the *Federation Proceedings* came across my desk with an interesting paper. It reported that patients with tumors of the adrenal gland excreted large amounts of what is called vanillylmandelic acid, which has methyl groups attached to the oxygen.[11] This gave me a clue. Since this tumor makes large amounts of noradrenaline and this compound, excreted in the urine, is closely related to adrenaline, it might be an intermediate

Figure 13.

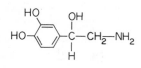

Norepinephrine

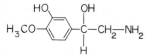

Normetanephrine

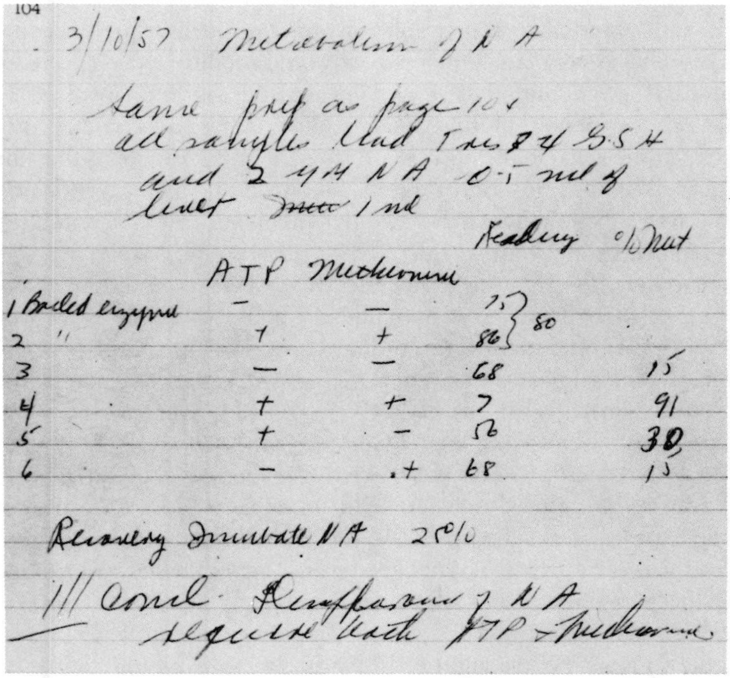

Figure 14. Page from laboratory data book: adrenaline experiment.

methylated noradrenaline, which we called normetanephrine [fig. 13]. I said, "that's interesting, perhaps noradrenaline goes through an O-methylation pathway." That very afternoon I realized that in order to form this compound, you have to have a methyl group donating compound. And the way methyl groups are transferred to other compounds is through an amino acid, methionine. But, methionine has to be activated to S-adenosylmethionine. I didn't have any S-adenosylmethionine, but I knew that it could be made by ATP and methionine.[12] Also, I had a method for measuring adrenaline.

That day I did a very crucial experiment [fig. 14]. I added noradrenaline (NA), some liver extract, ATP, and methionine, and measured the disappearance of adrenaline. The more it disappears the lower the number gets. I found that adrenaline disappeared, but only when I added ATP and methionine. When I left out either one, there was very little disappearance. I knew I had it. I knew I had a new enzyme and a new metabolic pathway for noradrenaline.[13] In a few months I worked out the metabolism of adrenaline and noradrenaline, norepinephrine, as it is called in this country.

I knew that noradrenaline is a neurotransmitter and I wanted to find out what role this newly discovered enzyme plays in the inactivation of noradrenaline. One important property of a neurotransmitter is that its action has to be terminated very fast. Otherwise, it would produce these effects for a long time. It was found that if we blocked the enzymes involved in noradrenaline, the action of the noradrenaline was rapidly ended. My collaborators and I felt, as in the case of other neurotransmitters, that the action required an enzyme—but it didn't. We were up against a problem. How do the sympathetic nerves that make noradrenaline end its action if the action isn't ended by enzymes?

Radioactive noradrenaline was synthesized for us. With a radioactive tag, tiny amounts of many kinds of compounds can be traced in the body. We injected radioactive noradrenaline into animals and found that it persisted long after its physiological effects had gone.[14] This indicated that noradrenaline was sequestered somewhere in the body.

The experiments were going well. It might sound like 1, 2, 3, 4, and always ask the right question next. Not so. I have notebooks full of experiments that were ambiguous and led nowhere. But sometimes things do work out in sequence. After several experiments we found that the injected noradrenaline was going directly to the sympathetic nerves. It appeared that sympathetic nerves specifically recognize and take up noradrenaline. We had to prove it, but we realized that if this was so, a neurotransmitter can end its actions by being taken up into the nerve and held there in an inactive form.

To test this, we destroyed the sympathetic nerves of a cat on one side by removing ganglia in the neck on one side. All the nerves on this side disappeared within two days, so the cat had intact nerves on one side and no nerves on the other. We injected radioactive noradrenaline, and most of it went to the innervated side; the denervated side had very little radioactivity.[15] We knew it went into the nerve, but then we had to prove it by other experiments.[16] Figure 15 is the radioautograph of the sympathetic nerve after injection of radioactive noradrenaline. From these uptake experiments, a new way of thinking opened up about sympathetic nerves.[17] It led to the discovery of the actions of many drugs.

A little earlier there was a great revolution in psychiatry, as a result of the introduction of three types of psychoactive drugs that relieve schizophrenia, depression, and mania. This excited many of us, indicating that there is some biological cause for mental illness. If a chemical can relieve mental illness, there must be some biological cause for the disease. This concept led in the last twenty to thirty years to very rapid advances in our understanding of the chemistry of the brain and how drugs interact with the brain.

We wanted to link noradrenaline with one mental illness, depression. We knew that noradrenaline was going into the nerve and we had evidence that antidepressant compounds, which relieve the blues, had some effect on the nerves. We injected the antidepressant drugs and followed them by radioactive noradrenaline. Those drugs, which were active antidepressants, blocked the uptake of noradrenaline.

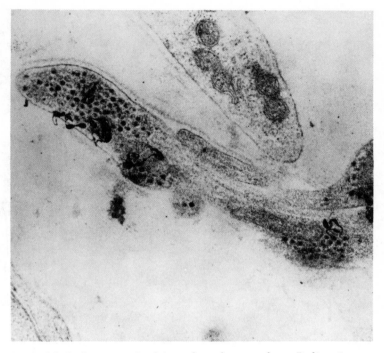

Figure 15. Radioautograph of tissue from denervated cat. Radioactive noradrenaline produces black dots on photographic film indicating its location.

Many drugs, such as LSD and mescaline, resemble the chemical structures of neurotransmitters and produce hallucinations. This led many neuroscientists to associate abnormal behavior with neurotransmitters.

Several years ago the Harvard botanist Richard Evans Shultes went into the Amazon and studied plants that Indians use for their own special religious rituals.[18] These plants produce very strange psychological effects, and the Indians believe they are communicating with their gods. One of these plants, *Virola calophylloidea*, called by the Indians Epéna, was used in a very sophisticated way. They dried the bark and administered it by forcibly blowing it right into the nose [fig. 17]. It produced unusual behavioral effects.

Chemists soon isolated the active principle of this plant and identified it as dimethyltryptamine [fig. 16]. Some of you are familiar with this as an hallucinogen, the so called "businessman's trip," since it acts so fast.

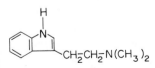

Figure 16. Dimethyltryptamine

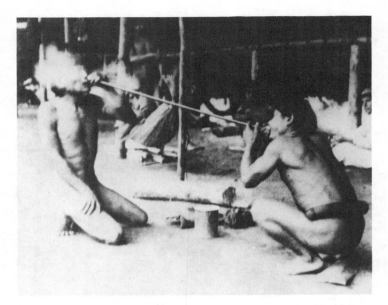

Figure 17. With a forceful blow, the intoxicating powder from the plant known to the Waika Indians as Epéna enters the nose.

In a reverie one day I thought of a way for looking for dimethyltryptamine in the body. I found it; at least I found enzymes that can make it.[19] But the funny thing is, the enzyme was present in the lungs. I don't know how the lungs can affect the brain, but it was there.

Research, of course, not only gives you pleasure, but it may help people too. About twenty-five years ago there were many people entering mental hospitals at an accelerated rate.[20] The dotted line in figure 18 gives the projected rate if there weren't any drugs for the treatment of mental illness. After the introduction of drugs in 1953, there was a very marked decline in the number of people entering. The extrapolated line was still going down in 1978.

One problem I've been interested in is a sort of romantic one. It's the pineal gland, which is situated between the two hemispheres of the brain and was thought by Descartes, the French philosopher and mathematician, to play a very important role in the body, since it is the only unpaired organ in the brain.

Descartes believed that the pineal has to do with perception and influences many physiological functions. He also called the pineal the seat of the rational soul, since it connected the mind and the brain. Until about twenty years ago people tried to ascribe a physiological role to the pineal gland. Lots of confusing experiments were carried out until the isolation by Aaron Lerner of the active principle of the pineal gland, a compound he named melatonin.[21]

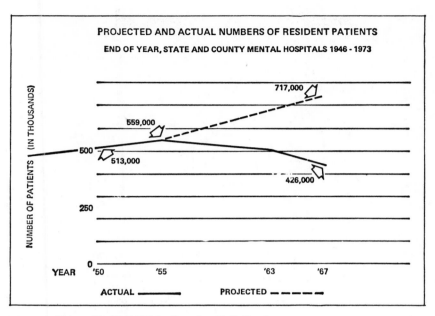

Figure 18. [© 1970 by Prentice Hall, Inc.]

We set about to find out how melatonin is made and what it does. After many years of work we found that the pineal functions as a biological clock. It produces a burst of melatonin every twelve hours in the absence of light.

When sympathetic nerves liberate noradrenaline, a receptor on the outside of the cell membrane is stimulated, which generates a second messenger, cyclic-AMP; this in turn stimulates the synthesis of a specific enzyme to form melatonin [fig. 19]. This finding is just the tip of the iceberg, and the function

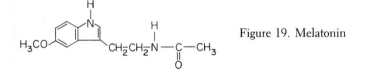

Figure 19. Melatonin

of the pineal is still a fascinating problem. For young people, it's one of the nice problems to do. It's sort of an off-beat problem and there isn't too much competition. You don't have to worry about priority, which many scientists worry about.

I'd like to tell you where the state of the art is right now on neurotransmitters. Figure 20 portrays what we know about the nerve now. It's terribly complicated. There are not only two or three transmitters, as was thought a few years ago, but also dozens of transmitters that have just recently been discovered [fig. 21]. There's noradrenaline, GABA, endorphins, encephalins,

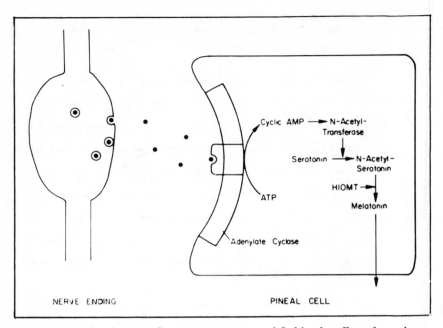

Figure 20. Mode of action of a transmitter is exemplified by the effect of noradren-aline on a pineal cell. Noradrenaline (dots) released from a nerve ending binds to a beta-adrenergic receptor on the pineal-cell surface. The receptor thereupon acti-vates the enzyme adenylate cyclase on the inside of the pineal-cell membrane. The activated adenylate cyclase catalyzes the conversion of adenosine triphosphate (ATP) into cyclic adenosine monophosphate (AMP). The cyclic AMP stimulates synthesis of the enzyme N-acetyltransferase; the enzyme converts serotonin into N-acetylserotonin. This is transformed in turn by the pineal cell's specific enzyme, hydroxyindole-O-methyltransferse (HIOMT), to form melatonin, the pineal-gland hormone that acts on the sex glands. [© 1974 by Scientific American, Inc. All rights reserved]

thyroid-releasing factors, and many more. I think this is just the beginning—and this is just one neuron.

There are ten billion or more neurons in the human brain, so there's lots of work to be done. I think these problems are soluble; it will take time, money, hard work, and enthusiasm for research.

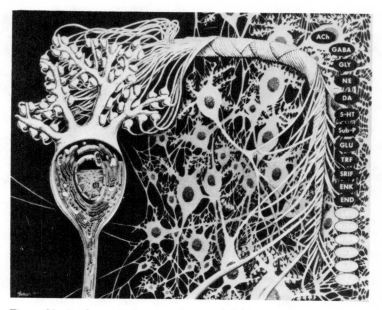

Figure 21. A schematic diagram of a neuron with some of the known neurotransmitters. [©1970, 1974, 1978 by Oxford University Press, Inc.]

Mathematics

I. M. SINGER

Norbert Wiener Professor of Mathematics, Massachusetts Institute of Technology; visiting professor of mathematics, University of California, Berkeley; member, National Academy of Sciences; recipient of Bocher Prize, American Mathematical Society, 1969.

"My inclination toward intellectual pursuits was encouraged by my English and chemistry teachers in Central High School, Detroit. I majored in physics at the University of Michigan (1941–44), but regret not availing myself of their marvelous mathematics department. Puzzled by both relativity and quantum mechanics, I tried to master these subjects while serving in the U.S. Army. . . . Having failed, I concluded I needed a year in mathematics before I returned to physics, and I became a graduate student at the University of Chicago in 1947. That year stretched to thirty. . . .

"In 1962, while a Sloan Fellow, I visited Oxford, England. . . . Michael Atiyah and I discovered an index theorem that combined topology, geometry, and elliptic partial differential operators in a new way. Our results extended, unified, and gave insight to some older theories. Exploring the consequences of this startling combination of different fields has kept us busy since then. Deep new applications continue to be discovered. Some of the most interesting . . . are in high-energy theoretical physics. Mathematicians and physicists now realize that underlying gauge theories is the mathematical structure of fibre bundles. As a result, global geometry has application to elementary particle physics, and at the same time physicists are asking many new geometric questions. It is exciting to search for the answers."

Dr. Axelrod and I live in different worlds; yet, as you will see, our attitudes toward research are similar. I was pleased to accept the invitation to come and speak at this symposium because I thought it was a beautiful idea to celebrate the centennial of Einstein's birth with a gathering of scientists and artists, discussing the joys of research. Most of us university professors are accustomed to talking, but usually within the narrow confines of our own specialty. I've never before lectured on personal matters like my own emotions toward research. But I thought, let's give it a whirl. It's something new; try it.

I must say, however, that I was shaken up as I prepared this talk. Last month I reread articles Einstein wrote—essays I hadn't read for a long time. I had forgotten how much he meant to me—how much of my life he had guided. I am not referring to Einstein the physicist, though even in science he has influenced me; chances are I'm closer to his work in my own than most of you in the audience. As a matter of fact, I gave my first series of talks on relativity forty years ago to a high school science club. I can't imagine what my peers thought of me at the time; it took me twenty years to understand what I was talking about.

It's a spiritual Einstein who really guided me and, in fact, in a way guarded me. I had an experience similar to Dr. Axelrod's. After several years in the army (having majored in physics as an undergraduate, specializing in infrared spectroscopy), I had an opportunity to run a spectroscopy laboratory. I turned the job down, to the shock of my friends and family, to return to school and pursue the search for truth that Einstein had instilled in me.

For example, here's what he wrote upon coming to the United States to live:

> To be sure, nature distributes her gifts unevenly among her children, but there are plenty of the well endowed, thank God, and I'm firmly convinced that most of them live quiet, unobtrusive lives. It strikes me as unfair and even in bad taste to select a few of them for boundless admiration, attributing super-human powers of mind and character to them—this has been my fate and the contrast between the popular estimate of my powers and achievements and the reality is simply grotesque. The awareness of this strange state of affairs would be unbearable but for one pleasing consolation. It is a welcome symptom in an age which is commonly denounced materialistic that it makes heroes of men whose goals lie wholly in the intellectual and moral sphere.
>
> This proves that knowledge and justice are ranked above wealth and power by a large section of the human race. My experience teaches me that this idealistic outlook is particularly prevalent in America, which is decried as a singularly materialistic country.

Let me quote, in part, another typical Einstein statement:

A hundred times every day I remind myself that my inner and outer life are based on the labors of other men living and dead, and that I must exert myself in order to give in the same measures I've received and am still receiving. The ideals which have lighted my way and time after time have given me new truth to face life cheerfully have been kindness, beauty and truth. Without the sense of kinship with men of like mind, without the occupation with the objective world, the eternally unobtainable in the field of art and scientific endeavors, life would have seemed to be empty."

I read such things when I was a teenager and determined that I would follow in his footsteps. What shook me up in preparing this talk was the conviction that I had failed. I don't mean the failure in one's work. Only a youth could hope to accomplish what Einstein did; most of us have to drop that dream very quickly in order to survive. I mean the failure of manner. We have not pursued research with the peace and spiritual grace of Einstein.

We are here to discuss the joys of research. Since my attitudes toward research have been influenced by Einstein, mine are close to his. He said, "one of the greatest wonders and mysteries of the world, one of the things we don't understand about the world, is that it is understandable."

He talked often about the joy of being able to contribute to our understanding of the world. I quote from a speech he gave honoring Max Planck, who formulated the concept of the quantum:

In the temple of science, there are many mansions, and various indeed are they that dwell therein, and motives that have lead them thither. Many take to science out of a joyful sense of superior intellectual power. Science is their own special sport to which they look for vivid experience and the satisfaction of ambition. Many others are to be found in the temple who have offered the products of their brains on this altar for purely utilitarian purposes. Were an angel of the Lord to come and drive all the people belonging to these two categories out of the temple, the assemblage would be seriously depleted, but there would still be some men of both present and past times left inside.

Further along he talked about the motivation of the men who are left inside:

"To begin with, I believe with Schopenhauer, that one of the strongest motives that lead men to attempt science is to escape from everyday life with its painful crudity and hopeless dreariness from the fetters of one's own ever shifting desires. With this negative motive there goes a positive one. Man tries to make for himself, in the fashion that suits him best, a simplified and intelligible picture of the world. He then tries to some extent to substitute this cosmos of his for the world of experience and thus to overcome it. This is what the painter, the poet, the speculative philosopher, and the natural scientist do each in his own fashion. Each makes his cosmos and its construction the pivot of his emotional life, in order to find in this way the peace and security which he cannot find in a narrow whirlpool of personal experience."[1]

My own motivations for doing research are: first, the private joy in the exercise of one's talents. When I was a youngster I envied many around me. They had much talent. There were those who could play musical instruments well and those who were good at sports. (A great tragedy of my youth was that I couldn't hit a curve ball!) I found, however, that I seemed to be able to think more abstractly than most. When I learned about science and mathematics as a teenager, I discovered that the manipulation of abstract objects, their construction, and their rearrangement, were things I could do very well. Exercising this talent has always been a joy.

Second, I find great satisfaction in creativity, for I then feel a kinship with artists and scientists the world over. A Matisse exhibit thrills and inspires me. I rush home and attack my own research problems with zest, feeling I am part of the world of Matisse. A good ballet affects me the same way. I love it, and am inspired to go home and try to do my little bit—like the juggler before the gates of heaven.

Third, research gives meaning to my life in allowing me to contribute to society in the only way I know. My contribution happens to be conceptual, in pure mathematics. An extra bonus lies in the special nature of mathematics, combining abstraction and applicability. It is amazing how often thinking abstractly and seeing new structures has important consequences.

I would like to illustrate this exceptional characteristic of mathematics: how the pursuit and development of intrinsic structures have surprising external consequences. It would be nice to take an example from my own work, but it is too technical and not far reaching. Instead, let me turn to history and describe how non-Euclidean geometry was developed from plane geometry.

About twenty-one-hundred years ago, Euclid wrote what was probably the most successful textbook ever written, *The Elements*. In it he systematized Euclidean geometry. It contains postulates and axioms from which one can deduce all of plane geometry. Most of you have struggled with the subject— and a few enjoyed it—in high school. One of the postulates, the fifth, or parallel, postulate, says: "Given a straight line, and a point off it, there is one and only one line through that point parallel to the original line." Parallel means that however long you extend the line, it never meets the original extended line. That postulate seems obvious and innocuous. However, even Euclid recognized that it differed from the other axioms and postulates. The others are especially simple. For example, "two lines can intersect in at most one point." Or, "given two distinct points, there's one and only one straight line through them." Euclid recognized the special nature of the parallel postulate by placing it late in his *Elements*. He developed as much geometry as possible before introducing the fifth postulate. Only when he needed to prove that the sum of the interior angles of a triangle is 180 degrees did he introduce the parallel postulate.

Geometers wondered about the fifth postulate. Could it be proved from the others? Was there a more obvious, simpler postulate that could replace the fifth and give the same results? These questions were asked about 270 B.C. and no one could answer them. For 2,000 years, mathematicians struggled with the parallel postulate and tried to prove it.

Finally, about 1820, three mathematicians—Bolyai, a Hungarian, Lobachevsky, a Russian, and Gauss, a German—independently developed an entirely new geometry, called hyperbolic geometry, in which the parallel postulate was false.[2] This new geometry is as consistent as Euclidean plane geometry. What a remarkable development! Plane geometry comes from the Egyptian surveyors, was systematized by the Greeks, and makes perfectly good intuitive sense. Centuries of questioning the fifth postulate led to a new geometry conceptually different and, at the time, unintuitive. Nevertheless, hyperbolic geometry had important consequences.

In 1830 Gauss discovered the geometry of surfaces. His student Riemann developed higher-dimensional geometry in the 1860s. By 1890, Felix Klein, professor of mathematics at Göttingen, had systematized the different kinds of plane geometry: Euclidean, elliptic, and hyperbolic. The full machinery of differential geometry was in place by 1900. In 1905 Einstein discovered special relativity and in 1916, general relativity. Special relativity, motivated completely by physical considerations, might possibly have been discovered without the previous geometric developments, but surely general relativity could not have been.

This story illustrates the point I made earlier: a theoretical development so very long in the making had an enormous impact. Non-Euclidean geometry altered the very way we think about the shape of the universe.

My story illustrates several other points. We do research in a social climate and that climate affects the way we think. I said that non-Euclidean geometry was discovered about 1820; as a matter of fact, it was discovered one hundred years earlier by a Jesuit priest, Gerolamo Saccheri, professor of mathematics at the University of Pavia. We all know cases of discoveries occurring earlier and not being recognized. But here even Saccheri didn't realize what he had accomplished.

He said, "Let's negate the fifth postulate." That would mean that through the point, either there are no lines parallel to the original one, or there are many. If there are no lines, he very quickly arrived at a contradiction. Encouraged, he assumed there were many lines through the point. Saccheri slaved away for years trying to arrive at a contradiction, for that would show he had proved the parallel postulate. Instead, he found strange results from his point of view. In fact, what he found were the theorems of non-Euclidean hyperbolic geometry. Eventually, he threw up his hands in despair and said, "I have failed." One hundred years later the three mathematicians I cited followed the same path. They threw up their hands and exclaimed "Eureka!" Actually, two of them said, "Eureka!" The third one was too chicken to say anything, as I'll shortly explain. Bolyai and Lobachevsky claimed they had discovered a new geometry. Mind you, they didn't prove that it was self-consistent. They simply asserted, "No one can find a contradiction. We've really found a new geometry."

It was Gauss who was chicken. Bolyai's father was a geometer and a good friend of Gauss. They'd been students together at the university in Göttingen. Bolayi the elder was proud and excited about his son's results. He immediately sent a letter to Gauss describing them. Gauss was hardly magnanimous in his reply. Unfortunately, I couldn't find the exact statement of his reply in the library, but it went something like this: "If I honor your son, it would be like honoring myself, for I too have found this new geometry. However, I felt it wise not to disclose it to the public, because it would be ill-received." Gauss was frightened of the prevalent philosophical position of the times. Immanuel Kant had said, "Our mind *a priori* perceives Euclidean geometry. There can be no other." Of course, Bolyai the younger was furious, because he felt that Gauss was trying to take credit from him. My second point is, then, that mathematics like any other science is done in a social context and is a very human activity.

My third point is that ideas are subtle and their transmittal may be subtle. One oftens hears about simultaneous independent discoveries; in this case I can't resist speculating that they may not have been truly independent.

I mentioned that Bolyai the elder was a friend of Gauss and that they had been students together at Göttingen. I didn't mention that Lobachevsky's teacher [Johann Bartels, University of Kasan] was also a friend of Gauss. Perhaps these three young men, Lobachevsky's teacher, Bolyai's father, and Gauss sat drinking beer one day, talking geometry. One of them may have said, "You know, maybe no one can prove the parallel postulate; perhaps if you negate it, you would just have a different geometry." That idea could have been implanted and buried in their minds. They dispersed and the idea ultimately came to light. Hyperbolic geometry was soon to come; for given that idea, any expert in geometry could follow Saccheri's path.

It might be helpful to describe what it's like to be a pure mathematician, because we are thought of as a breed apart. Not so long ago at parties, even faculty parties, if you said you were a mathematician, there was a shocked silence. People would say, "Oh, God, I barely got through trig." Or, "Calculus was about the most I could manage." Things have changed. Nowadays, an economist comes up and is pleased to tell me how well he knows the Lebesgue integral and talks about integrating over infinite dimensional spaces. A chemist describes how important the representations of orthogonal groups are in the study of the oscillations of a complicated molecule. Things *have* changed; nevertheless, we are still thought of as a breed apart. In many ways we *are* different.

How? For one, we don't need a laboratory or equipment; pencil and paper will do. We can work anywhere, anytime, though libraries and colleagues are important. I illustrate that by a personal story. Almost twenty years ago, I was awarded a Sloan Fellowship [for basic research]. I took the blurb that goes with it seriously. It said that I had no duties and I didn't have to write a final report. I was grateful for the gift of a year to pursue some ideas and to write a long paper. I chose to work in isolation on the Isle of Capri. It's a beautiful island. The tourists were gone and it rained a lot. There was no television. There were no movies, no dances, no sports. I tried to write my paper. I also pursued my marvelous ideas.

Day after day I'd walk and work on my paper, but the writing went poorly. I'd think about my marvelous ideas, but they led nowhere. After a month, I was desperate to talk to other mathematicians. I kept working on the paper and soon found I needed a library. I could reproduce some things I required, but there were known results I needed for my paper that I could not figure out for myself.

After three months, I gave up in desperation and after Christmas headed for Oxford. During our stay on Capri my wife had embroidered a beautiful piece of cloth. As we left the island, I said, "I think that's the most productive thing we did on this island."

But the time in Capri wasn't wasted. My mind rested. There's a famous joke about Oxford and Cambridge, filled with professors resting their minds, some of them for fifty years! I rested mine and came to Oxford eager to talk and eager to work. The rest paid off.

Oxford's Mathematics Institute now has a modern building. At that time, its offices were in a small house with an annex down the street. Since I had come at such short notice, I was put in the garret of the annex. On my first day, as I sat huddled over a heater, my good friend professor Michael Atiyah climbed the stairs and greeted me. He sat down and asked me a question. Why did a certain computation in topology lead to a whole number, an integer, where one expected only a fraction? Well, a theorem showed it to be an integer and Michael wasn't asking how to prove the theorem, he was asking a deeper question, a very searching question: Why should it turn out to be an integer?

I listened politely and went back to the lousy manuscript I was trying to complete. But that question kept gnawing at me, week in and week out. I found that I couldn't finish my manuscript (I seldom can) and ultimately abandoned it to think seriously about the question Michael had asked.

I was still on sabbatical and had lots of leisure. I remember many afternoons sitting with pencil and paper in the gardens of St. Johns, scribbling and thinking about "why an integer?" It finally occurred to me that the computation under consideration might be the answer to an entirely different question, which asked, "how many ways could you do something?" If you ask, "how many ways," that must be an integer. Perhaps these two questions in two different fields gave the same answer. One question led to the computational formula; one insisted the answer was an integer. I told Michael my conjecture and that set us working. We soon found that my conjecture was correct and we had linked two different fields in a surprising new way.

Further consequences of that liaison between topology and analysis still appear. Michael's question was a question of "wonder" about the internal structure of the subject. Yet there have been unexpected applications outside of mathematics. What we did fifteen years ago is now having applications in elementary particle theory. That should not be surprising, since the "index theorem" I have just spoken about involves the Dirac operator of physics and global differential equations of geometry.

Since this symposium is trying to look at the subjective life of a scientist, I will close with a description of how a pure mathematician goes about his research. At least how this one does. I have described what I did and didn't do on sabbatic leave. What is it like normally? I find my habits have changed with age. When I was younger, research life began about 11:00 p.m. Everyone around me was asleep and I could begin to work. The wonderful thing about beginning at that hour is that work is open-ended. I could simply continue for as long as I was able, ending at four, five, or six in the morning. I would pick up ordinary life again about noon: go to school, teach a course, attend a committee meeting, talk with colleagues, listen to a seminar, browse in the library, and so forth.

Of course, when I say 11:00 to 6:00 or 11:00 to 4:00, I wasn't always working. I read many mystery stories and novels. But my focus was the problem, or the combination of theoretical, abstract objects I was dealing with. There are different kinds of mathematicians. I for one am not a good computer. However, if I am really entangled in a problem and a computation is necessary, I can manage. I'm not a problem solver and I'm not good at chess. Nor am I good at puzzles. However, if a particular theoretical issue hinges on a special problem, then I'll attack that problem with enthusiasm. Often one fails, and as Dr. Axelrod said, "you have to know when to stop." When I stop, after success or failure, I pick up a novel or a mystery story and bury myself in it.

That's what research life was like for me up until ten years ago. For reasons I don't understand, it is different now. Perhaps age and added responsibilities caused the change. Those of us who have had some success in research are called upon to do all sorts of things (like lecturing at the Smithsonian). We take on more than is consistent with research. I now try to set aside afternoons and no longer work at night. Frequently, if I'm excited about a special problem I will get up about 3:00 a.m. and work for two or three hours. It would be nice to say that each afternoon I concentrate on my research, but I don't think I average more than three days a week. There are too many other obligations. That's one of the ways I have failed old Albert.

But I am fortunate to be able to participate in the program he initiated. Let me explain. I remarked that the development of non-Euclidean geometry was essential to general relativity. Most of you know that during the last thirty years of his life, Einstein sought a unified field theory for electromagnetism and gravity. He failed to find it. I believe one reason he failed is that the geometry he needed hadn't been developed yet. This geometry, global geometry, involves fibre bundles,[3] characteristic classes, and elliptic analysis. It has enjoyed an enormous growth in the last forty years.

Quantum field theory is now using global geometry in gauge theories;[3] in fact, high-energy physics and geometry enjoy a new liaison, which began in 1977. Physicists are trying grand unification schemes once more, though not the way Einstein did. It may turn out that global geometry will be essential to a unified field theory. The next ten or twenty years should also show whether ideas of global geometry will be useful in explaining the strong forces holding the nucleus together. I am, of course, very excited about these developments, as excited as I was when I gave my first lectures on relativity.

Axelrod-Singer Discussion

ANNA J. HARRISON, Moderator

Emeritus William R. Kenan, Jr., Professor of Chemistry, Mount
Holyoke College; past president, American Chemical Society and member of the board of directors; board of directors, American Association for
the Advancement of Science. Research in molecular spectroscopy and
photolysis in the ultraviolet and far ultraviolet regions of the spectrum.

Participant: I think it's a common theory in an American institution of
research that, given enough time and enough money, especially enough
money, almost any question you might ask, if you asked the right question,
would be solvable. Do you really believe that?

AXELROD: No, I didn't mean to say that. Throwing money at a problem
will never solve it, if the time is not right. There are many, many instances
I might cite, possibly our present program of trying to solve or get a cure
for cancer by throwing a lot of money at the problem. If the time isn't
right, the *Zeitgeist*, as Dr. Singer says, you can't solve the problem. What
you need is a proper atmosphere. You need the right people. You need
money, that's necessary, at least with the type of extensive technology
required to solve the problem. All the easy problems have been solved
cheaply. Now you have the tough ones, which are expensive. Money
alone will not do it. You need more than that. You need proper

environment, freedom. I think if somebody tells you, "I want to solve this problem, in this particular way," it just can't be done. The time has to be ripe for a solution.

SINGER: Just think of the Greek government putting money into the parallel postulate problem.

Participant: If the Greek government had put more money in, then science might be different. What is the responsibility of those countries now that really can afford to pay the salaries of a Professor Axelrod, a Professor Singer, and all the other scientists needed? When we come to think of it, there are really relatively few countries that can afford the luxury of maintaining a Pythagoras. The Greeks were relatively prosperous in those days. This allowed people the time to think. But how about all the other cultures in the world that don't have this luxury? Do we have an added burden, therefore, as one of the few prosperous countries, to continue to support the people in developing countries who may have the same clever brains that we have in our country, but not the opportunities? What is your reaction?

SINGER: I think one of my points was that mathematics has this two-fold thrust. It's part of the humanities. It's part of a cultural activity. As such, it should be supported just like heart research and music are supported. To the extent that we have a viable society, its cultural activities are extremely important. Luckily for mathematics, it also happens to have serious applications and, therefore, can be supported on that basis too.

AXELROD: I wonder what the motives are of this present government for supporting science. I think they have been mostly political. Before World War II, there was very little support of science—and science for its own sake. I think it was the atom bomb that altered its support of scientific research. The government felt that if science could win a war, it could do lots of other things for the benefit of the country. I doubt whether support of science by the government, at least, is purely to gather information for aesthetic reasons. I think there are practical reasons involved for this support. It is believed that extension of knowledge will prove to be useful and do some things. There was another burst of support after the Sputniks. Here the reason was again purely political.

Participant: Since students' interest in science seems to be the thing that is nurtured in high school, I wonder if you would address yourself to opening up possibilities for summer research fellowships for high school students who are very, very interested in getting into this sort of thing: the possibilities of perhaps government money or universities making these opportunities available to gifted students.

AXELROD: I think that is very important. The initial impression of a good laboratory, a good atmosphere for young persons, would have a very important impact in their subsequent careers. There *are* programs. I know of one in the Jackson Laboratory for high school students to do summer research.[1] There are programs also at various universities. What one has to do is seek them out and find them. There should be more such support.

SINGER: I concur. However, there is a difference between the theoretical sciences and the laboratory sciences. You can absorb students in laboratories and they can be part of the activity. On the theoretical side, it's a little difficult. With computer sciences, it might be possible. By and large, it is difficult to get a high school student, even an undergraduate in college, involved in research activities in theoretical sciences, as far as I can see.

Linus Pauling: I was disappointed in Professor Singer's talk. Pleased in a way with it, but still disappointed because I didn't learn what he's working on. Last Christmas, I was talking with an outstanding mathematician, a French-American mathematician. I asked him what he was working on and he said, "I couldn't explain it to you." I said, "Well, can't you make a try?" He said, "No." I said, "I took half a dozen courses from Bateman on integral equations and things.[2] Don't you think you could give me an idea?" He said, "No." I said, "Does it have anything to do with number theory, perhaps prime numbers?" He said, "Yes." I said, "What?" He said, "well, I'm afraid I couldn't explain it to you." I said, "Why?" "I don't know how to start," he said, but "if I come back to California next year, I'll think about it in the meantime, and, perhaps, I will think of a way to explain to you what I'm working on."

This matter of counting up the number of ways in which something can be done, *that* interests me. I just wonder if Professor Singer could give me a *little* idea of what he's working on![Applause]

SINGER: In my defense, I had been given only half an hour. I decided it was impossible to try and explain. Given only one minute, I can manage. If you take certain partial differential equations and you ask for the number of independent solutions, that's an integer, a whole number. It turns out in geometry that you can express that number of solutions by an integral formula over the manifold on which that solution lives. That is, over the domain in which the functions of solutions live. That integral formula involves the geometry of that manifold. It involves the data given by the partial differential equation, and so the theorem I'm alluding to says that the number of independent solutions is given by a complicated integral formula, which you can check explicitly in many cases.

HARRISON: Professor Singer, you have used two words, both of which have some meaning to me, but you put them together. I suspect that the combination doesn't have any meaning to me at all; that's *global* and *local geometry*.

SINGER: Yes. What I mean by *local geometry* is what's happening in a small region. It can be a large region, but it's still a region. *Global geometry* is, for example, living on a sphere, or living on a torus, the surface of a tire. A question of global geometry is whether our universe is open or closed, which we still don't know. Life is different if you are living on a closed global surface or if you're living locally. It's the development of global geometry over the last forty years that has been spectacular and seems to be having applications in quantum field theory.

Participant: Not a question, but a comment. While Professor Singer was telling of his difficulties, in isolation on Capri, without library facilities, without contact with other mathematicians, I was reminded, with awe, of Einstein. In his fantastically seminal year in 1905, his papers overthrew the world of physics. He was living in Berne, working forty-eight hours a week as a patent clerk, without time even to get to the inadequate library in Berne, and had no direct contact with any theoretical physicists. It wasn't until 1909 that he first went to a physics conference where he first met another theoretical physicist. Professor Singer's experience has pointed out the unbelievable nature of Einstein and why he really was legendary.

SINGER: Yes, we're not all Einsteins.

AXELROD: I would like to pursue this, Dr. Singer. What was the critical influence in 1905 for Einstein proposing these three fundamental physical laws or discoveries?

SINGER: I don't know the intent of the question.

AXELROD: Something must have triggered his thinking, just at that time.

SINGER: The situation in physics was that electromagnetism, Maxwell's theory,[3] was really a revolution that hadn't been properly understood. Forces were transmitted by fields instead of at a distance and that really was diametrically opposed to Newton. Einstein, in his genius, understood that it was a revolution and fought his way back to fundamentals in order to try and understand what the implications of Maxwellian theory were. In addition, there was Planck's famous 1900 paper, postulating the existence of the quantum in order to explain blackbody radiation.[4] For reasons that I don't know, except his sheer genius, Einstein was able to understand the implications earlier than other people.

AXELROD: But it didn't appear to many famous physicists at that particular time. They didn't seem to recognize this.

SINGER: As usual, you can go back and see ghosts of the development elsewhere. Even the idea of black holes is several hundred years old. LaPlace[5] computed the mass that a star would have to have to prevent light from escaping it. From Newton's laws, somebody in the early nineteenth century computed that light would have to bend as it grazed a star. In fact, this computation was the same one Einstein made in 1909 that was wrong by a factor of two because he hadn't developed general relativity yet. Already, Lorentz[6] had some of special relativity, Poincaré[7] had some of special relativity, but not from the purely physical principles Einstein used.

Participant: First a comment and then a question. All the sciences are indeed the humanities. I know this flies in the face of the dictum of a famous man, Lord Charles Snow,[8] who complains about two cultures and rightly so. I think there is a basic fallacy, if Lord Snow actually means fully what he says, that there's a terrible dichotomy. What characterizes science is that it has so much in common with the arts and the other humanities. It has an aesthetic quality.

However, Professor Singer, you have explained the general idea of global geometry. Would you try to sketch how it is that it affects elementary particle physics?

SINGER: As to your first comment, I agree completely. As far as I'm concerned, science is part of the humanities. It's part of our culture. I've always felt that way. I only emphasized mathematics because it's my home base.

Now, as to how these global considerations enter into field theory, I'll try and give you two examples. Let me talk to the audience in general.

There are certain nonlinear differential equations that are coming up in what's called "gauge theories" of quantum field theory.[9] One would like to see what the solutions to those equations look like. Classically, we would like to know, because they are the base around which you make quantum fluctuations. All this is happening in our space time, or in Euclidean space. If you analyze the solutions to these equations as you go out to infinity, they look bad. On the other hand, if at infinity, you twist the space (I can't really describe that, just feel it), they look simple. Think of the solutions as functions on the plane. Think of infinity as going to the South Pole. At the South Pole, twist the space we're talking about. Knot it up; then the solutions look very nice on that globalized space. So what looked like a fairly complicated solution in the ordinary plane, say, everything but the South Pole, with this twist becomes fairly elementary. The way to study a solution, or the space of solutions, is to allow for those possible twists. Analyzing the twists is a branch of global geometry, or topology.

Another example goes back to Dirac.[10] It's called the Dirac monopole, in which he derived the existence of a quantum for electric and magnetic charge from the existence of one monopole. This monopole had to have a singularity at a point. It turns out that again, if you twist the whole space, as you come into that point, there really isn't a singularity there. You can extend the solution to the twisted space in a nice way and there is a solution to these nonlinear problems in a way that one hadn't imagined as little as ten years ago.

HARRISON: I hope that answer also pleased Professor Pauling. [Laughter]

Participant: Dr. Axelrod, when you outlined your scientific history you emphasized "being at the right place at the right time and talking to the right people." How do young people find the right place and the right people, is it a matter of luck? How did you just happen to be at the right place at the right time?

AXELROD: It's both a matter of luck and seeking out. What happens to many scientists is that there's a very recent discovery and it's very exciting. Most scientists rush in to work out the details of that discovery. One has to anticipate where it's going to be and try to sense where the developments are. For example, right now I'm working on a problem of structure of membranes. How do signals get through membranes? This is a very important problem in biology. It's very complicated. In the course of this work, I had to learn a lot of immunology, which was pretty strange to me up until about two years ago. I asked people, "who's a good immunologist? Who can I talk to? Who can bring me up to the state of the art in immunology and who can I discuss ideas with?" That's one way of doing it.

Another is to ask for the right articles to read, the right type of literature, and to attempt to fit in your new ideas with this information. It's very hard to give pat formulas. Everyone has his own style of working. One works better one way. Most people find it impossible to work the way I do. And so, one has to fit one's own style, personality, the resources available, etc. You just can't give a patent type of formula to be a success.

HARRISON: I'd like to make one comment to students in that connection. I think part of this is looking and expecting opportunities to occur. Try to recognize it when it's there. You may have a very fixed wall or preconceived plan for your life. When something deviates from that, you may not recognize it for the opportunity that it is.

George Field: I've been thinking about our educational system and whether Einstein would have approved of it. One of the things he did relentlessly throughout his life was to pare away and discard those activities that were unimportant. He focused solely on the things that he considered to be important. Does our educational system do that?

The other is that he wrote, I believe, a strong attack on our system in which each faculty member is expected to produce at a certain rate, what we would now call a publish-or-perish syndrome. His own view of how to do the best scientific work, which he applied early in his life, as we have heard, at the Patent Office, was to find a job that was not too demanding. It should be coupled only weakly, if at all, to one's own professional interest. In one's spare time, so to speak, important interests could be pursued.

Is our academic system responsive to Einstein in that respect? Both of our speakers this morning have exemplified this to a certain extent. Professor Axelrod talked of his own achievements attained, remarkably enough, *in spite* of the educational or professional system through which he was traveling. He paused to take the Ph.D. degree only because it was necessary. Professor Singer alluded to his leaving the important work until after 11:00 p.m., which is an open-ended time for him.

My own feeling is that our educational system does not encourage the creative impulse to the degree that it should.

Participant: I also am concerned about the early development of young scientists. What is the extent to which the breadth of the early experience is important in your later career? Neither of you was a standard student, who decided at age sixteen to be a plasma physicist, did nothing but study plasma physics for the next twenty years, and then produced wonderful results. In my own career, it was very valuable to have done chemistry as a high school student and experimental physics as a part-time job as an undergraduate before I got into theoretical physics and geometry. Would either of you comment on the breadth of life experience in the early stages?

AXELROD: I did what I did in spite of the educational system. I think one has to have a certain enthusiasm, an indomitable spirit. Genius and creativity are very rare things. They are not very commonplace. Even among good scientists, there are few that are really creative. I would guess 10 percent of the science done has an impact and is very creative. It's very hard to say what type of education will make a really outstandingly creative person.

Einstein is an example. He did it in spite of the type of situation. As a patent office examiner who worked forty-eight hours a week, he did it. I don't know whether one can educate people in a very formal way to become really productive and creative scientists. I'm a little gloomy about it; I just don't know. It's a matter of luck, a matter of genes, a matter possibly of not being suppressed too deeply so that you give up.

SINGER: I think what you're asking is, why don't we have more guts? Remember, we're all fallible. Suppose Einstein hadn't made those discoveries that first year. Suppose he had been free from the usual academic duties and went on trying for twenty years. I wonder how he would have fared. My point is: our educational system in a sense reflects our own timidity. It's very hard to try and work on something, to fail, and to have nothing to show for it. That's why people often don't try hard. They might still fail. You must have some substitute activity such as teaching, committee work, or what have you.

I don't know what to tell young people. The educational system doesn't stand alone in this. Our whole social structure as such asks people to follow certain routines. By the time students reach high school, their attitudes about following these routines are pretty much settled. If they're lucky, they will find a teacher here or there who exemplifies an entirely different approach, I don't think a system can exemplify it. What we can do is encourage individuals to set an example of creativity and hope that those individuals will populate our school system as teachers so that young people can see and feel creativity and originality.

HARRISON: I worry about the filter our educational system imposes on students. Those people who are successful in our educational system early on in the sciences seem to have two qualities in particular. They must have them in order to get the recognition that encourages them to stay. One is that they can absorb a large quantity of material rapidly, and the second is they can reply quickly to clever questions in a limited amount of time. Neither of these are the qualities that you are looking for in the individual who is innovative or creative. It disturbs me lest our educational system is filtering to exclude the very innovative and the very creative.

Participant: Professor Singer, what was the basic conflict that Einstein had with the quantum theory? Some of his ideas were based on Planck's work, and his photoelectric effect was a quantized idea.

SINGER: Einstein said, "God doesn't play dice." He felt that quantum mechanics was a statistical description that was limited and didn't describe the real world. He didn't believe in the uncertainty principle, for example, though he understood its practical significance. I believe there's an exchange of letters between Bohr and Einstein on just this point.[11]

Participant: I'm a student who is considering going into research. At what point in your life did you realize that research was the career for you and that you had something to contribute. How did you realize that? When and in what way did you suddenly say to yourself, "I think I'll stay in research for the rest of my life?"

AXELROD: I think I gave that in my lecture. However, for most, for a person like yourself, I think the most critical time is right after graduate school, when you have what is known as a postdoctoral fellowship. There, it's important to be in a really first-rate laboratory, if you're interested in laboratory research. Try to get a postdoctoral fellowship in a very active laboratory. There you are thrown in with a lot of young people who have just finished their graduate training. There you can test your mettle. You find out if you can work as an independent investigator. This is the most important thing.

Participant: Basically, what you are saying is that you have to kind of proceed into the field. Only then do you see whether you're being successful or not in coming up with innovative questions.

AXELROD: Yes, it takes a long time to really come out with something very outstanding. It takes taste, judgment, experience, which you have to learn.

I learned that I wanted to do research purely by accident, as I said, when I was thirty-three. I hadn't had any intention of doing research, but when I did, I knew it was what I wanted to do. But most people don't do it this way.

Participant: Dr. Singer, is that route the same for you, too?

SINGER: I'll tell you my experience, but I'd like to warn you that times are different now. I think young people are in a much more stressful situation vis-à-vis research than we were.

I kind of backed into it. First of all, I was a physics major as an undergraduate. I almost majored in English instead of physics. I didn't, simply because it was clear that many of my fellow students felt and understood poetry much better than I did. I made a second choice, which was physics. I took a course in relativity and quantum mechanics. I was, as Einstein was, upset with quantum mechanics. I simply didn't believe what I read and what people told me. I then spent several years in the army carrying along with me a book on quantum mechanics and a book on geometry so that I could understand relativity. When I got out of the army, I decided to go to graduate school and planned to spend only one year in mathematics because I felt I needed that background to understand these two subjects. That one year lasted forever, so to speak. But again, I was always pursuing trying to understand something. The idea of doing research with a capital R never occurred to me. I was just trying to understand something. What I found over a period of time was that if I thought hard about something, I often understood it better than other people—to the point where I could explain some things to other people. Sometimes I could explain things that nobody had seen before. That's how I got into research.

Participant: I'd like to comment on how science it being taught to us in the high schools and what the system, as it is presented to us now, seems to be. In my school, it is required that we take two courses in the sciences, the basic courses. One is Introductory Physical Science and the other one is Biology. After that, it's left up to you. Most people are not discouraged from taking other sciences, but it's not really encouraged. My school concentrates more on English literature and liberal arts.

If you want to go into research, or medicine, or any of the sciences, you must take all the courses you can in high school and then try very hard to get into a very good school. It seems this is the only way you're ever going to get anywhere. Once you get into school, you have to take the hardest courses. The courses are designed to be as hard as possible so that they will winnow out (that was the word used to me) people who can't make it. After that you spend years, you have to get grants, and you try and get a job. It's almost an endless process. It seems almost impossible to get anywhere unless you are very brilliant or you're very lucky.

SINGER: What you're saying is there's no joy in research. [Laughter]

AXELROD: Yeah, you're probably right. However, I think you have to have the spirit. You just don't give up. You try and again you try to seek the opportunities. Remember that many, many people are getting into research. It's hard. You have to seek out money. That's very important. It's very expensive to do research. If you're good, you can make it, but if you are very good, it's easier.

SINGER: I feel that what you've described is very tragic, but I don't see a way out.

HARRISON: I worry about this, because I think it's not so much the *difficulty*, but the element of *adventure* that doesn't come over. I look at a course in physical chemistry, or something of that sort, and I think we don't really play fair with the younger people. I think what went on this morning is an offset to that. In class you have all of these nice derivations and they follow one right after another. Some way or another the idea comes across that this is the way science developed. It didn't. It developed in a very erratic manner. After one has all the bits and pieces, someone who is good at writing a textbook can line it all up and make it look like it just proceeds in this fashion. It doesn't! The fun of it is the chase.

Participant: I'm a graduate student in physics. Einstein said something to the effect that he didn't really know what the universe was all about, but that when we found out, it would appear simple and elegant. It seems as science progresses, especially in biology, things become more and more complicated. Do you see any synthesis of knowledge or coalescence appearing as Einstein predicted?

AXELROD: Not in the biological sciences, I don't. It's too complicated, too complex. I tried to give you a feeling for this. However, I think it's understandable. Although things are complicated, they're understandable, ultimately. It's very difficult to get elegance in biology as one gets it in physics, except possibly the Watson-Crick theory of heredity.[12] That's exceedingly rare.

SINGER: In physics, I think Einstein's right. I think ultimately the universe will appear very simple. But, of course, that simplicity depends on a certain kind of knowledge. I, for example, get a thrill everytime I teach in the calculus, the derivation of Kepler's laws,[13] planetary motion coming from the inverse square law of Newton. To me this is a high point of human civilization.

But you have to know the calculus to be able to understand it. Once you know the calculus, it's very simple. I think Einstein's point, too, is that when you really see through the deep structure, it will turn out to be very simple. In fact, the present day attempts at unified field theory are really enormously simple.

Participant: While I was listening to the lectures, the thought kept going through my mind that serendipity must have played an important role in your lives. Is that so?

AXELROD: Oh yes, it plays an important role for all scientists. As Pasteur said, "in the field of observation, chance favors only the mind that is prepared."

SINGER: The unprepared one as well!

Oncology and Virology

HOWARD M. TEMIN

At the University of Wisconsin, professor of oncology. Wisconsin Alumni Research Foundation Professor of Cancer Research, and American Cancer Society Professor of Viral Oncology and Cell Biology; editorial board, *Journal of Virology*; member, National Academy of Sciences; winner of Nobel Prize for Physiology or Medicine, 1975.

"I received my elementary and high school education in the public schools of Philadelphia. My specific interest in biological research was focused by summers (1949–52) spent in a program for high school students at the Jackson Laboratory in Bar Harbor, Maine, and a summer (1953) . . . at the Institute for Cancer Research in Philadelphia. . . . My first laboratory [in the McArdle Laboratory for Cancer Research, University of Wisconsin] was in the basement, with a sump in my tissue culture lab and with steam pipes for the entire building in my biochemistry lab. Here I performed the experiments that led in 1964 to my formulating the DNA provirus hypothesis. . . .

"Now I am primarily studying the formation of retrovirus DNA and its integration with cell DNA and the evolution and origin of retroviruses."

Biologists probably are not usually thought to have been influenced by Einstein, but I too, as a youngster, was inspired by his life. So I am pleased to participate in this symposium. I am also pleased that this symposium is at the Smithsonian Institution, for it and the Franklin Institute in Philadelphia played important roles in encouraging my interest in science.

Joy is not present in science as an everyday thing. What is customary is satisfaction. Therefore, in this symposium I want to emphasize the satisfactions—and frustrations—of present-day basic biomedical research.

In particular, I would like to contrast what we were able to do in virology more than twenty years ago when I was a graduate student (one of whose professors was Dr. Pauling) and now. In 1956 I started work with Rous sarcoma virus,[1] which causes cancer in animals and foci of altered cell morphology in cell culture. We showed that these foci were analogous to tumors. The question we were interested in was "how does Rous sarcoma virus cause cancer?" The only techniques available then were counting the number of foci and securing what we called "growth curves." That is, seeing how rapidly virus is produced [fig. 22].

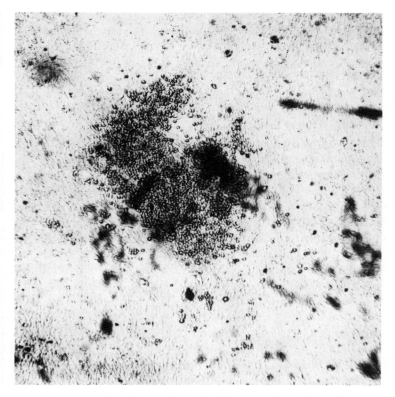

Figure 22. Focus of chicken embryo fibroblasts transformed by infection with Rous sarcoma virus ten days previously.

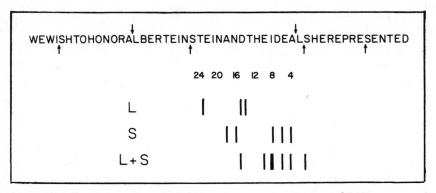

Figure 23. Illustration of concept of restriction enzyme mapping of DNA.

From these types of experiments, which were called by some of my bacteriologist friends a "primitive kind of cytology," we could only make indirect guesses at the answer to our question. The framework for our answers was what is called the "Central Dogma of Biology," that is, DNA makes RNA makes protein.[2]

With the techniques that became available in the last twenty years, we have shown that the general form of the answer to the question "how does Rous sarcoma virus cause cancer?" is that the virus adds to the cell genome a specific gene that causes cancer. In doing so it violates the Central Dogma. More specifically, it is now possible to specify in molecular terms, that is, in terms of DNA sequences, exactly what is added and where it is added.

I want to show you how we can specify in such detail things like that. Two major techniques are used—restriction enzyme mapping and DNA sequencing.[3]

Restriction enzymes are agents that cut at a specific short sequence of DNA. To illustrate, let us imagine a specific sequence of letters as shown in figure 23. If we cut at each L and then separate the cut sentence by the number of letters in the fragment, we find out how far apart the L's are. If we then take another enzyme that cuts at S and repeat this procedure, we find out how far apart the S's are. Finally, if we cut with both enzymes together, we find out how far the S's are from the L's. We thus can start to "map" the sentence—indicated by arrows in figure 24.

In actuality, we work with DNA, a linear message of four letters, and we use very sensitive methods involving radioactive isotopes, electrophoresis, nucleic acid hybridization, and autoradiography to map picogram quantities of DNA; that is, the equivalent of the amount of DNA in a single cell or in 100,000 small viruses. The map positions are thousands of letters apart. These map positions can be used to tell how the virus sits in the cellular DNA.

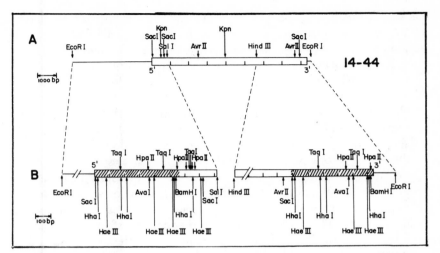

Figure 24. Restriction enzyme cleavage map of cloned provirus of spleen necrosis virus. A is a representative cloned molecule (14-44); B represents detail of ends of provirus. Straight line is cell DNA; open bar is provirus; crosshatched bar is long terminal repeat of provirus. [© 1980 by Macmillan Journals, Limited]

To get more detailed information about the DNA, we use nucleotide sequencing methods [fig. 25]. To do this, we read from one point in a message to each repetition of a letter. At each repetition, we stop and go

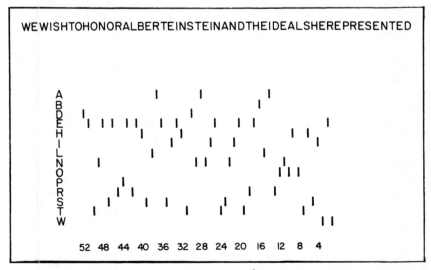

Figure 25. Illustration of concept of DNA sequencing by base-specific methods (dideoxy or Maxam-Gilbert techniques).

back to the beginning, reading from the beginning to the next repetition of a letter. We repeat this process for each letter. For each letter we then separate the messages stopped at each repetition of that letter. Thus, for each letter we determine how far it is from the beginning of the message and we can read the message. This technique works for small quantities of nucleic acid.

This capsule history of one field shows the framework for my satisfactions in research. Part of these satisfactions are for the whole field and part for myself, an individual scientist. Twenty years ago, I could not have dreamed of the extent of our present ability to ask and answer specific questions about biological systems. Furthermore, in telling this story I can see my specific contributions, ideas, and reagents. The major satisfactions are having new insights, developing new understandings, and opening new fields for study. There are also the more frequent satisfactions of making new observations, doing clean experiments, and interacting with other scientists as a peer and as a teacher.

Occasionally, there are those special moments in research that might be called joyful. Last week, for example, we thought we succeeded in getting an animal virus we work with to grow in bacteria by use of the techniques of recombinant DNA or genetic engineering. With this apparent success, I realized we could answer questions that we had been trying unsuccessfully to answer, questions that had not been possible to answer previously. Furthermore, the availability of these clones opened to me whole new questions and areas to study. I felt much was now possible that had previously been only wishful thinking.[4]

But more and more the satisfactions of research are being overlaid with frustrations, which are both on an individual level and on the level of the field and even science in general.

Some frustrations are endemic to science and are the counterpart of the satisfactions. I mean not being clever enough, not being quick enough, not being bold enough, not receiving sufficient credit for a new finding, not being the first to describe something, and not having significant consequences come from a discovery. These frustrations have always been in science and always must be if it is to remain a creative and individual endeavor.

I am not referring to these frustrations, but to new external ones. United States biomedical science has become hindered by an overintrusion of regulations. The newer problems can be summarized as insecurity, over-regulation, and unnecessary bureaucratization, and an erratic appreciation of research and its results. Insecurity includes the need to worry how each experiment will look to grant-reviewing committees, whether others are doing the same experiment, whether the results will have immediate significance, and what the future conditions for research will be. Over-regulation and bureaucratization include detailed regulation of radiation safety, of chemical safety, of chemical carcinogens, of recombinant DNA, and of percent effort applied by the scientists to a grant, as well as stringent fiscal, hiring, and personnel controls.

I will illustrate these frustrations with two examples. One is the question of the causes of human cancer. Because of the fear of cancer we have large antipollution efforts by government. For example, in McArdle Laboratory, the cancer research laboratory where I work, we must spend tens and hundreds of thousands of dollars to insure that no one is exposed to carcinogenic compounds. Yet research has shown convincingly that cigarette smoking is the major preventable cause of death from cancer.[5] And little is done by the government to discourage cigarette smoking. More could be done educationally and by using taxes to discourage smoking of high-tar and nicotine cigarettes.

Another illustration is in the area of recombinant DNA research. The numerous techniques involved in this field have revolutionized the study of the genome of higher organisms and enabled the powerful techniques I described before to be applied to higher organisms. Use of these techniques has already led to a major and surprising discovery.[6]

The genes of bacteria and of vertebrates are fundamentally different in organization. From a practical point of view, this difference essentially removes a whole class of previously conceivable hazards of recombinant DNA experiments, namely, that random cloning from a vertebrate cell could lead to expression of harmful genes in bacteria. However, a large body of regulations still governs our experiments with this technique, and what experiments have been done depended much more on what country a scientist worked in and the nature of the regulations than on what was scientifically best.

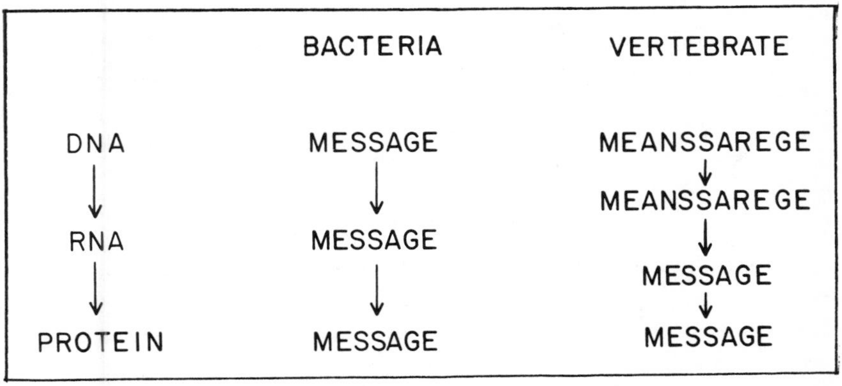

	BACTERIA	VERTEBRATE
DNA	MESSAGE	MEANSSAREGE
↓	↓	↓
		MEANSSAREGE
RNA	MESSAGE	↓
↓	↓	MESSAGE
PROTEIN	MESSAGE	↓
		MESSAGE

Figure 26. Information flow from DNA to protein in bacteria and vertebrates. In vertebrates the RNA message for proteins has intervening sequences that are removed from the RNA after its synthesis.

We also fear that this kind of regulation is increasing. More of our time and research funds are spent coping with safety regulations whose effectiveness and benefits are not apparent and with bureaucratic regulation designed to make administration simpler and having the effect of making research less effective.

Science is one of the noblest constructs of our age. It has changed all of our lives and provided unique opportunities to a fortunate few people. The trend I see is that the effectiveness of science and scientists is being curtailed. The gains from this curtailment are not always apparent. There are still important things to be learned in science and great satisfaction in being a scientist. I hope that the children born in this year of Einstein's Centennial will have the same opportunities in science that we have had in the last 100 years.

Theoretical Astrophysics

GEORGE B. FIELD

Professor of astronomy, Harvard University; director, Harvard-Smithsonian Center for Astrophysics; editorial board, *Astrophysics and Space Science*; president, Commission 34 (Interstellar Matter), International Astronomical Union; executive committee, NASA Space Advisory Council; fellow, American Physical Society; chairman, National Academy of Sciences-National Research Council Astronomy Survey.

"It was the books of the famous English astronomers Sir James Jeans and Sir Arthur Eddington in the local library in Edgewood, Rhode Island, that got me started. *The Stars in Their Courses* and *The Universe Around Us* [among them] were beautifully written expositions of the mystery of space and time.

"Several people made particularly deep impressions on me. Professor Earl Coddington of MIT in a course on mathematical analysis established a standard for logical rigor that was not forgotten. George Gamow . . . at George Washington University lectured engagingly and provocatively on nuclear physics and thermodynamics. My chief mentor was Professor Lyman Spitzer of Princeton. . . . the world's leading authority on interstellar matter and on dynamics of star clusters, the initiator of controlled fusion research in the United States and the inventor of the Copernicus ultraviolet satellite and of the space telescope now under construction by NASA. . . . Early in my career I [also] worked with Professor Edward Purcell of Harvard, . . . [whose] willingness to share his rich . . . knowledge about physics was a major stimulus. Finally, I was fortunate to have lived in Princeton during Einstein's last years and was his next-door neighbor at the time he died. Like many scientists at the time, I wept openly on hearing of Einstein's death. This man, perhaps without my knowing it, had come to symbolize the beauty of science. . . ."

When Einstein showed how the paradoxical results of the Michelson-Morley experiment could be understood by adopting a completely new theory of space and time, he was expressing in the simplest mathematical terms the facts forced on us by that experiment.[1] From the power of this new theory—the theory of special relativity—one would have to conclude with Einstein that "the eternally incomprehensible thing about the world is its comprehensibility."[2]

When he posited that gravitational fields are governed by his famous equation $G_{\mu\nu} = T_{\mu\nu}$, which constitutes sixteen nonlinear partial differential equations for the sixteen components of the tensor $G_{\mu\nu}$ representing gravity, Einstein seemed to be going far beyond what the facts warranted.[3] True, these equations of the theory of general relativity reduced in the appropriate limit of small velocity to Newton's theory of gravitation. And the equations expressed the same principles involved in special relativity, albeit in a vastly expanded arena. But the equations of general relativity represent an inspired guess as to the nature of gravitation nevertheless.

Sir Arthur Eddington (1882–1944) was a British astronomer whose great contribution was showing how the energy production of the stars could be explained naturally in terms of the physics of gases at high temperature. He was also one of the small band of astronomers who was excited by the implications of Einstein's new theory of gravitation for astronomy. In spite of the intervention of World War I, he was instrumental in mounting a British expedition to South America in May 1919 to look for the deflection of starlight by the sun during an eclipse, one of the three classic experimental tests of general relativity proposed by Einstein. The close agreement of observation with theory was an astonishing vindication of the theory, and of the comprehensibility of the world. I'll return later to a very recent test that goes right to the heart of general relativity.

Eddington wrote superb books about astronomy for the layman.[4] I came across them in the local library in Edgewood, Rhode Island, when I was in junior high school. These books revealed for me the beauty of the universe and of the laws describing it. Eddington spoke of stars and galaxies, vast agglomerations of matter in an enormous expanse of space, obeying precisely the laws of physics of Newton, Planck, and Einstein. I was intrigued then with the adventure of trying to understand the astronomical universe.

I was fortunate to be admitted to the Massachusetts Institute of Technology in 1947. The physicists there, who had developed radar and the bomb during the war, were eager to apply their new techniques to studying atoms and nuclei in the laboratory. I very much enjoyed my mathematics and physics courses, but it was frustrating that MIT had no courses in astronomy. I began to realize that galaxies were more interesting to me than atoms.

After graduating from MIT, I spent a year in Washington, D.C., and thus had an opportunity to hear George Gamow lecture at George Washington University. Although he was teaching nuclear physics and thermodynamics, he talked a lot about his research on molecular biology and the origin of the chemical elements in a big-bang universe. At last I was getting into astronomy. At my request, Gamow provided a reference for me to get into graduate school at Princeton. Characteristically, his reference consisted of a one-line remark scribbled on a postcard.

Princeton in 1952 was the world's leading center of theoretical astrophysics. Lyman Spitzer, a specialist in interstellar matter, and Martin Schwarzschild, a specialist in stellar structure, were making models of stars and interstellar clouds employing a broad range of physical principles—nuclear and atomic physics, thermodynamics, and the theory of gravitation. My studies between 1952 and 1955 with Spitzer led me toward studies in interstellar matter.

Just before I went to Princeton, Edward Purcell, a physicist at Harvard, and his student Harold Ewen had succeeded in detecting radio emission by hydrogen atoms in interstellar space.[5] This emission, caused by the flipping of the electron from a state in which its spin is parallel to that of the proton to one in which it is antiparallel,comes out in a very narrow band of wavelengths near 21 centimeters. Using their little antenna projecting from a window at the Jefferson Laboratory, Ewen and Purcell were able to detect, by using the Doppler effect of the emitting atoms, the rotation of the entire Milky Way galaxy, whose radius is 30,000 light years [figs. 27 and 28].

This discovery set me thinking. If one could thus map out the rotation of the galaxy, hydrogen atoms in intergalactic space would enable me to map out the expansion of the universe. At the April 1955 meeting of the American Astronomical Society (AAS) held in Princeton, I recall discussing this possibility with David Heeschen, then a young researcher at Harvard and until recently the director of the National Radio Astronomy Observatory. He encouraged me to undertake it, and I did so starting in June 1955 when I went to Harvard as a postdoctoral fellow.

That April is vivid in my mind. I was finishing my Ph.D. dissertation at Princeton and gave my first paper at the AAS meeting on my findings. At that meeting Bernard Burke and Kenneth Franklin announced their unexpected discovery that the planet Jupiter is a powerful radio source. And just a few weeks before, Albert Einstein, who happened to live in the house next door to mine on Mercer Street in Princeton, had died.

Harvard was great. On the one hand there was a radio telescope fitted for 21-cm work, which had free time available. And Purcell generously advised me on calculating something very important to know in understanding my results: to what degree the atoms were excited by various processes. For a typical atom in intergalactic space, excitations can occur via collisions with other atoms, collisions with free electrons, absorption of photons at 21-cm

Figure 27. The radio "horn" used in 1951 by Harold Ewen and Edward Purcell at Jefferson Laboratory, Harvard University, to detect 21-centimeter radiation arriving at the earth from hydrogen atoms in the Milky Way. Radio waves entering the horn are amplified and the resulting signal is recorded in the laboratory.

wavelength, or fluorescence initiated by absorption of Lyman-α photons at 1216 angstroms.

While working at the radio telescope part of the day, I spent the rest of the time calculating each of these processes. The rate of absorption of 21-cm photons depends upon the intensity of such radiation deep in space, something one might hope to measure directly with a radio telescope. I remember discussing this possibility with Ewen, and his advising me that it would be technically very difficult with the equipment than available. I'll come back to this point later.

The search for intergalactic hydrogen produced a null result, but I could put an interesting upper limit on its density using the theory I had developed for the excitation.[6] This led others to try the experiment; it has not been detected to this day, in spite of great improvements in instrumentation.

After my encounter with intergalactic space, I went back to interstellar research, developing the theory of interstellar clouds and studying their stability. Because the Milky Way is slowly evolving, with new stars constantly forming from interstellar clouds, study of interstellar matter has become a major branch of astronomy. In pursuing these studies I was intrigued to read

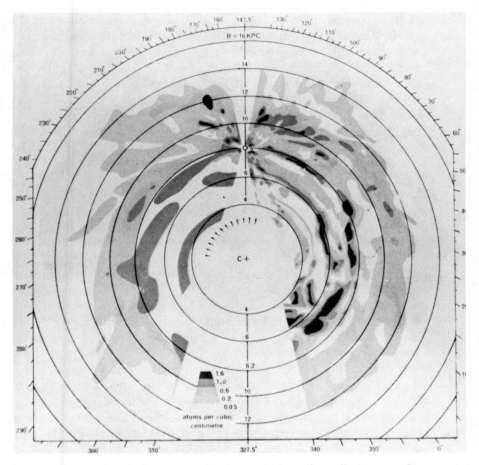

Figure 28. A map of the distribution of hydrogen atoms in the Milky Way, made by using the 21-centimeter radiation they emit. The atoms are located by the Doppler shifts in their 21-centimeter emission. Note the concentration into spiral arms, proving for the first time that the Milky Way is a spiral galaxy.

about an unsolved astronomical problem in Gerard Herzberg's book on diatomic molecules.[7] In 1941 Andrew McKellar had identified two closely spaced lines of the molecule cyanogen (CN) in the spectra of distant stars.[8] Apparently the CN lay in interstellar space, far from any stars. The curious thing was that unlike excited states of other interstellar atoms and molecules, the $K = 1$ rotational level of CN was excited enough so that an absorption line arising from it was observed, along with the line from the $K = 0$ ground level. On page 496 Herzberg writes, "From the intensity ratio of the lines with $K = 0$ and $K = 1$, a rotational temperature of 2.3° follows, which has of course only a very restricted meaning."

For me the meaning was clear: it simply meant that the various processes capable of exciting $K = 1$ in space had balanced out at a population ratio that could be formally expressed in terms of a "rotational temperature" of 2.3°K, using the Boltzmann equation applicable to level populations in thermal equilibrium. Thus, one should be able to derive the 2.3° figure from the rates of the various excitation processes.

I set out to do this, in the same way I had done for hydrogen, by estimating cross sections, etc. However, in calculating the rate at which CN would absorb photons at a wavelength of 2.6 mm (the wavelength of the $K = 1$ to $K = 0$ rotational transition), I needed to know the permanent dipole moment of the molecule, and this had not yet been measured. Even rough estimates, however, indicated that CN in the $K = 1$ level would quickly radiate, depleting the $K = 1$ level faster than it could be excited by collisions or fluorescence. Of course, just as in the case of atomic hydrogen, any photons of 2.6-mm wavelength would excite the molecule, and in the limiting case when emission and absorption of such photons occur much more frequently than other processes, the populations would come into equilibrium at a temperature equal to the thermodynamic temperature of the radiation at 2.6-mm wavelength. In thinking about this, I could not imagine any source of such radiation. So I wrote up what I had done in a draft paper and filed it; this was about 1963. Too bad, because I had missed the cosmic blackbody background radiation about which more later.

The very earliest rocket flights instrumented to detect cosmic x rays suggested the presence of a diffuse background coming in more or less equally from all directions. Gold and Hoyle suggested that the universe is filled by intergalactic gas heated to 10^9 K by the β-decay of neutrons created *ex nihilo* in their theory of the steady-state universe.[9] Gould and Burbidge calculated the x-ray intensity on this model, and showed that it would greatly exceed that observed.[10] In 1964 I realized that the same effect would occur in big-bang cosmology if some agency like quasars heated the gas, and with Richard Henry calculated expected x-ray spectra.[11] Since then observations at the wavelength of Lyman-α have shown that the density of intergalactic atomic hydrogen is extremely low; any gas present must be ionized, so the interpretation of the x-ray background as emission by hot gas is plausible. Recently, a student and I derived $T = 4.4 \times 10^8$ ° K for the temperature of the gas required, and about half the density for closing the universe as its density.[12] [See figure 29.] Hence, we can now understand why the early attempt to detect hydrogen atoms failed: the gas is completely ionized.

Arno Penzias and Robert Wilson of the Bell Telephone Laboratories were awarded the Nobel Prize in physics for their 1965 discovery of a ubiquitous low-level field of thermal radiation in the universe. In his book *The First Three Minutes* [New York, 1977], Steven Weinberg discusses how it happened that this discovery was accidental despite the fact that it had been predicted from a theory of element formation in big-bang cosmology by Alpher and Herman.[13]

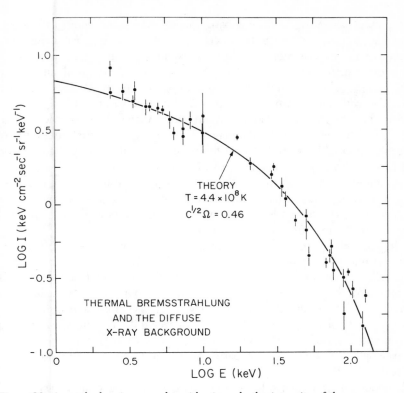

Figure 29. A graph showing on a logarithmic scale the intensity of the x-ray background radiation coming from deep space, plotted against the logarithm of the energy of the x-ray photons involved, from 1 kilo electron Volt (keV) to more than 100 keV. The dots are experimental points; the vertical bars represent the errors of measurement. The curve represents the x-ray background that would result from hot gas between the galaxies whose temperature is 400 million degrees Kelvin, and whose density is about half of that required to close the universe. [© 1977 by University of Chicago Press]

Penzias wrote his Ph.D. thesis at Columbia under the supervision of Charles Townes. His subject was one that I had worked on earlier: the search for extragalactic hydrogen using 21-cm techniques. Later, in 1963, he became interested in the background intensity of radiation at 18-cm wavelength, because of the excitation it would cause in interstellar OH molecules for which he was searching. I remember our discussing this question in my office. Little did either of us realize, however, that some years later he would make such a measurement (at 7-cm wavelength) which would result in his winning the Nobel Prize.

In about 1964 Robert Dicke of Princeton instigated a search for background radiation in the centimeter wavelength region, having realized that it should be present according to the big-bang model. As I was teaching an under-graduate astronomy course at Princeton in 1965, I remember seeing on a roof outside the classroom in Palmer Laboratory the apparatus to carry out this experiment being set up by his collaborators Peter Roll and David Wilkinson. I also remember attending a colloquium by Jim Peebles, a theorist working with Dicke, who explained why the experiment was important. I recall thinking that Alpher and Herman had predicted the same effect. Thus in 1965 I was aware of the theoretical work of Alpher and Herman and of Peebles, and had myself discussed the possibility of measuring the radiation at 21 cm with Ewen and at 18 cm with Penzias. However, I failed to make the connection between the predicted blackbody radiation and the measure-ment of background radiation that would excite intergalactic hydrogen and interstellar OH. Nor did I recall the apparent need for radiation of some kind to explain the excitation of cyanogen in space.

In the summer of 1965 I had just accepted an appointment at Berkeley, and set out with my family by car to California. Even as we were enjoying the sights of the western desert, Penzias and Wilson were publishing their momentous discovery [fig. 30]. When I arrived at Berkeley, I learned of their paper,[14] and the accompanying one by Dicke, Peebles, Roll, and Wilkinson,[15] proposing that Penzias and Wilson had discovered the radiation from the big bang and emphasizing the importance of measuring its intensity at other wavelengths (as they were preparing to do at 3 cm) in order to test its blackbody nature.

Suddenly I remembered the CN problem. Perhaps the cosmic background radiation was responsible for exciting it. If so, a number of conditions would have to be fulfilled:

(a) The CN rotational temperature would have to agree with that measured by Penzias and Wilson, $3.0 \pm 0.5°$ K.

(b) The rotational temperature would have to be the same in all regions of space, and therefore, in all interstellar spectra in which CN appeared.

(c) The dipole moment of CN would have to be large enough so that emission and absorption processes at 2.6-mm wavelength would be faster than any other process affecting the rotational populations.

Remarkably, I was able to answer all these questions within a few weeks. On the first point, I knew only that Herzberg had quoted McKellar as giving a rotational temperature of $2.3°K$, slightly outside Penzias and Wilson's quoted error. But by coincidence I learned that a Berkeley graduate student in astronomy, John Hitchcock, had been analyzing the interstellar CN lines on some plates of the star ζ Ophiuchi taken by George Herbig of Lick Observatory. Stepping into his office next to mine, I learned that a better value for the rotation temperature in ζ Ophiuchi was $3.2 \pm 0.2°K$. Moreover, Hitchcock had data for another star, ζ Persei, which indicated $3.0 \pm 0.6°K$. In one stroke, my conversation with Hitchcock had yielded new information on items (a) and (b).

Figure 30. Dr. Robert Wilson (left) and Dr. Arno Penzias with the "sugar-scoop" radio antenna at Bell Telephone Laboratories with which they discovered the cosmic black-body background radiation in 1965. They were awarded the Nobel Prize for Physics in 1978 for this discovery. The intensity of the radiation they detected at 7-centimeters wavelength is equivalent to that emitted by a blackened surface at a temperature of 3 degrees above absolute zero. In spite of its low intensity, this radiation is believed to have originated in the explosion that occurred at the origin of the universe.

The other question was answered through an even greater coincidence. I had written an article on another subject for the *Annual Review of Astronomy and Astrophysics*, and to guide me in correcting galley proofs, the editors had sent me proofs from the previous edition. By Claude Arpigny of the Institut d'Astrophysique de Liége, the article was concerned with the spectra of comets, a subject I knew nothing about, but before dropping it in the wastebasket I had noticed that it mentioned CN, a prominent feature of such spectra. Thinking about the excitation of interstellar CN, I fished in the wastebasket for the galley proof. As I read, I could hardly believe my eyes.

Arpigny was reviewing his theoretical work on the spectrum of CN in comets, published the year before.[16] Apparently the CN lines undergo dramatic variations as comets approach the sun. These variations can be understood as the result of the competition between two effects—the increasingly rapid excitation of the various rotational levels of the upper electronic state by absorption of sunlight and the steady deexcitation of the rotational levels of the ground electronic state by rotational transitions.

The rate of excitation could be calculated from known parameters of the CN molecule, but the rate of rotational deexcitation could not be calculated because, as I had found earlier when working on the interstellar CN problem, the dipole moment of CN was unknown. However, Arpigny had made laborious calculations for each of several assumed values of the dipole moment and had been able to fit the observed line strengths with just one value, 1.2 Debye units. In short, he had measured the dipole moment of CN by observing its cometary spectrum.

When I put this value into my excitation equations I found that condition (c) above is indeed fulfilled. The story was complete. It was a great joy to tell this to the December 1965 meeting of the American Astronomical Society, being held in Berkeley;[17] more detailed accounts were given later.[18] Since then, additional data on the other stars have fully confirmed this work[19] and the dipole moment of CN has been measured in the laboratory to be 1.45 ± 0.08 Debye;[20] this somewhat larger value strengthens the argument further.

A great deal has been written on the cosmic blackbody radiation.[19] True, it had been predicted on the basis of the big-bang model. But couldn't something like it be produced even in the steady-state model? Many attempts to do so have been made, but so far most have foundered on the requirement that the radiation follow a strict blackbody spectrum. In all of these discussions, the CN point at 2.6 mm has played an important role because for a long time it was the shortest wavelength at which a measurement existed. In 1974 D. J. Hegyi et al.[21] observed another CN line arising from the $K=2$ level, getting a rotational temperature of 2.9 ± 0.5°K at a wavelength of 1.3 mm, on the short side of the blackbody peak at 1.8 mm [fig. 34]. This and the measurement of $K=1$ imply that the radiation cannot be "greybody," that is, because of hotter bodies occupying less than the whole sky, for in that case the radiation would be three and twelve times brighter, respectively, than indicated by CN $K=1$ and 2 populations. D. P. Woody et al. have verified the blackbody nature of the radiation over the range 0.6 to 2.5 mm and obtained T = 2.99°K.[22] [See figure 31.]

Einstein realized that his theory of general relativity permitted one to build models of the universe. In 1917 he published a model in which the universe was static.[23] In order to obtain such a model, however, he had to modify his original equations by the ad hoc introduction of a new term called the cosmological constant, λ. Later it was observed that the universe is actually expanding;[24] only then it was realized (by most American scientists at least) that the Soviet mathematician and meteorologist A. Friedmann had earlier derived models of an expanding universe from Einstein's original equations with $λ = 0$.[25] Einstein later regretted his introduction of λ,[26] and today it is largely regarded as unnecessary.

As far as I know, everything we know about galaxies and their motions, about the blackbody radiation, and about the abundances of the chemical elements, is consistent with Einstein's original equations and Friedmann's cosmological models based upon them. The outstanding question of the day is *which* of the Friedmann models is correct, the closed model, which has finite mass and volume and is fated to halt its expansion and recollapse to infinite density, or the open model, which has infinite mass and volume and will expand forever. [See figure 32.]

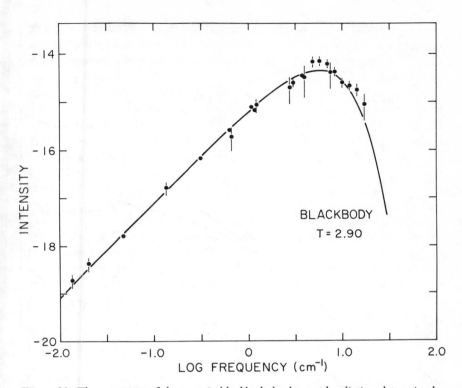

Figure 31. The spectrum of the cosmic blackbody background radiation determined by different experiments, plotted on a logarithmic scale. The logarithmic frequency scale is calibrated in units of waves per centimeter; the discovery point of Penzias and Wilson is the one a bit to the right of −1.0. The cyanogen point discussed in the text is located at about +0.5, where the theory (indicated by the curve) predicts a significant departure from a straight line. The curve is the theoretical best fit for blackbody emission at 3 degrees above absolute zero.

Both models are consistent with general relativity, but which one is correct depends on the amount of mass-energy present. More exactly, it depends on whether the density of matter-energy is greater (closed model) or less (open model) than 5×10^{-30} grams per cubic centimeter. The blackbody radiation contributes only 0.0001 of this; galaxies contribute 0.05 of it; and, if one believes the interpretation of the x-ray data, ionized intergalactic gas contributes 0.5 of it. One sees why it is important to know the latter number—and know it precisely. That is what I am working on.

Soon after his discovery of general relativity, Einstein examined his equations to see what effects might be predicted. As stated earlier, at extremely small velocities the equations reduce to Newton's, so the whole classical theory of the solar system is recovered. But if the small but finite velocity effects are included, small but finite differences from Newton's equations

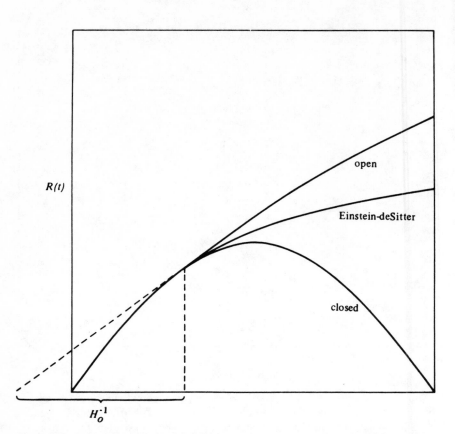

Figure 32. A. Friedmann's models of the universe. Time is on the horizontal axis, with the big-bang at the origin, and the present time (about 13 billion years if Hubble's constant is 50 kilometers per second for each mega parsec distance), indicated by the vertical dashed line. The three curves indicate how the size of the universe varies with time. If the present density is large enough, the universe is closed and is fated to recollapse, while in the opposite case, the universe is open and will expand forever. The dividing line is called the Einstein-deSitter model; in this case, the universe expands forever but reaches infinite size with zero velocity of expansion.

appear, and on this basis Einstein proposed three tests: the bending of light by the sun's gravitational field, the shifting toward larger wavelengths as the light climbs out of the gravitational field of a star or planet, and the slow movement through space of the line connecting the sun to the point in a planet's orbit that is closest to the sun. All three of these effects have been observed, and in all three cases the results agree with prediction to better than 1 percent (better than 0.01 percent in the case of the wavelength shift).

Einstein also predicted a completely novel effect: gravitational radiation.

Figure 33. A view of the Arecibo Observatory of the National Astronomy and Ionosphere Center, Arecibo, Puerto Rico. The edge of the 1,000-foot-diameter radio telescope appears at the bottom of the picture, while the "feed" that picks up the radio waves reflected to it by the telescope is seen in the upper-right corner. The feed and its associated electronics are suspended 600 feet above the antenna by a system of towers and steel cables.

Just as moving electrical charges emit the electromagnetic radiation that is so important to living things, rapidly moving masses emit gravitational waves that also travel at the speed of light. Such waves alternately compress objects in one dimension while stretching them in the other, then the reverse.

So far no one has ever detected such radiation. According to Einstein's equations, it would take huge masses moving at a good fraction of the speed of light to generate a measurable amount of radiation. Thus the collapse of an entire star into a black hole in a thousandth of a second would cause a bar one meter long on the earth to stretch a distance less than the radius of an electron! In spite of this, scientists have been working for over a decade to directly detect such radiation if it exists.

Now comes the news that such radiation has been detected indirectly via its effect on the orbit of an unusual double star, made up of two neutron stars orbiting in close proximity. Because one of the neutron stars is a pulsar, its motion can be traced with fantastic accuracy by radio astronomers using the big dish at Arecibo [fig. 33]. In so doing, it has been found that the period of the double star has shortened by 1.0×10^{-4} sec (out of 2.8×10^4 sec) in the four years since its discovery,[27] and this agrees precisely with the prediction by general relativity based on the fact that the rapidly moving masses are losing energy via gravitational radiation.

The march of science is exciting, even awesome. Einstein's insights were

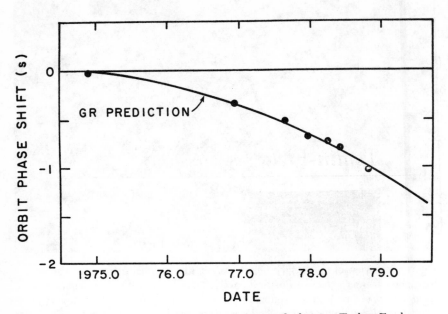

Figure 34. Verification of Einstein's general theory of relativity. Taylor, Fowler, and McCulloch (see note 27, George B. Field) carefully timed the arrival of radio pulses from a rotating neutron star, using the Arecibo Observatory shown in figure 33, and thus deduced that it is very slowly spiralling in toward a companion star to which it is gravitationally bound. The rate at which this should happen, as a result of radiation of gravitational waves, can be calculated from general relativity (line labeled "GR"); the calculations agree well with the observations (dots) showing that general relativity is verified. [© 1979 by Macmillan Journals, Limited]

of a fundamental order rarely matched in the history of science. His theory of general relativity, based on close reasoning but also involving a great intuitive leap, is turning out to be an accurate description of the world [fig. 34]. One again thinks of Einstein's own maxim concerning the comprehensibility of the world.

I have been lucky enough to be involved in the recent growth of astronomical knowledge. Those days when all the threads were coming together in the story of CN and the cosmic blackbody background were the most exciting for me. I think it comes down to this: for me, the joy of science is the beauty of nature as revealed in the simplicity of the principles that describe its inner workings. This means constant unification in theory of phenomena once thought disparate. Einstein achieved such unification writ large. The rest of us remember times, like my encounter with CN, when the nature of puzzling phenomena is suddenly revealed. Einstein said, "The most beautiful thing we can experience is the mysterious. It is the source of all true art and science."

Temin-Field Discussion

ANDRÉ E. HELLEGERS, Moderator*

Director, the Joseph and Rose Kennedy Institute for the Study of
Human Reproduction and Bioethics, Georgetown University; professor
of obstetrics-gynecology and physiology-biophysics, Georgetown, and
lecturer in population dynamics, Johns Hopkins University; consultant
on ethics, American Medical Association; editorial board, *European
Journal of Obstetrics and Gynecology* and *Concilium* (journal of theol-
ogy). Research in obstetrics-gynecology and fetal physiology.

* Dr. Hellegers died a short time after the colloquium at the age of
fifty-six.

Participant: I have an observation on Dr. Temin's remarks. About ten
years ago I was at lunch in Berkeley and found myself sitting next to a man
who recently had won a Nobel Prize. In those days at Berkeley, when you
won a Nobel Prize, they built a new building for you. This meant a
building had just been finished. I walked around it in the morning. It was
a round building and there was a curious wooden temporary building
leaning against it. When I found myself next to him at lunch, I asked
what that shack was leaning against his building and he said, "I don't
know, the English Department or something." I said, "You know a
hundred years ago, the English Department would have been in the new

building and the Chemistry would have been in the shack." He said, "That's probably right."

There's a difference, as Dr. Temin has discovered, between living in the big building and in the shack. You get more exposure in the big building. I doubt that you can enjoy the comforts of the big building while retaining the freedom of the shack. A hundred years ago, an English professor could get in trouble for writing free verse. It was a crime to split an infinitive, and if he used a four-letter word, heaven knows what would happen. The death penalty was still in effect in those days. Now the English professors are living in the shack and happy as clams. I think that has something to do with the predicament of the scientist today as mentioned by Dr. Temin.

TEMIN: One can assume that we're like King Canute, sitting at the sea as the tide comes in and saying, "stop!" I hate to believe, and certainly don't think it's a fundamental law of nature, that just because things are big, they have to be so bureaucratic and inefficient. I may be wrong, but we hope that there can be more decentralization and especially more effort where there are real problems. For example, returning to the issue of laboratory safety, we see there are real hazards in laboratories, like smallpox viruses. A smallpox virus-induced death tragically happened in England in 1977.[1] There are real dangers in the laboratory and world. I hope that we'll respond to real dangers and not to imaginary ones.

Participant: Both speakers emphasized that it's good to know when to stop in pursuit of something that is beginning to look hopeless, unobtainable. In the case of George Gamow, mentioned earlier, he also knew the converse. After having made the calculation Dr. Field described, proving that it was impossible for a computer to decipher the genetic code, he noticed at once the work of Crick and Watson when it came out and proceeded anew to try and decipher the genetic code. He made some progress. I hesitate to try to explain to this audience exactly what Gamow's contribution was, but it's rather remarkable that he did turn around and work at this, with some success. His great abilities as a physicist and cosmologist did not deter him from tackling even problems in biophysics.

TEMIN: The "coding problem" was a key one in genetics and Gamow did make an effort. Actually, many other very clever people in the 1950s also made great intellectual efforts to solve the problem of the genetic code. One of the most remarkable results that Gamow proved was that the code couldn't be overlapping.[2] Where there was a sequence of letters that described one message, it couldn't describe more than one message. This seemed to be a very elegant proof, and the total code, when everything was worked out, established that the code was nonoverlapping. Unfortunately, theory in biology doesn't count for too much.

First of all, none of this theory, except for the conceptual idea of a code, was used in the solution to the genetic code. The actual solution came about from straight biochemistry. To some of us, this was almost sad. It did not have the elegance of genetics. It was straight biochemistry, very brilliantly carried out originally by Nirenberg.[3] The code was resolved by straight biochemistry. Very recently, when Sanger's group, using techniques like the ones I discussed, actually sequenced an entire genome, a little circular genome of a virus named $\phi \times 174$, they found that the code was an overlapping one.[4] Since then, in several other viruses, where nature has put a great premium on using things as efficiently as possible, overlapping codes occur that Gamow had proved were impossible. Biology, fortunately or unfortunately, is an historical science and theory hasn't had that great a predictive value.

Participant: I'm an historian of science. Dr. Temin described how institutional constraints affect the freedom of science. As research gets bigger and more complex, how can we keep our institutions as creative as possible? What suggestions or recommendations would you make for keeping the home of science as creative as the shack, as well as being supportive as the large building described earlier?

TEMIN: I have to make a distinction as Phil Handler, the president of the National Academy of Sciences, made when he spoke recently about science and the future of scientists. Science, in terms of the results and the work coming out, I think, is incredible. In all the fields that I'm aware of, and in the newspapers, it seems that things are burgeoning. The sum of science is still extremely alive and extremely creative. However, for an individual going into science, there are real problems. There's going to be much more winnowing, as the high school student stated earlier. There are going to be many fewer who are going to make it through and become scientists. The only thing that I can think of in relation to this is that we are in an era of limited resources. We have more scientists being produced than there are jobs. We also have more science being produced now than there ever was before. We're concerned to use the limited resources available to do science rather than the other kinds of things I referred to. However, there are still young people coming up who, in spite of these great institutional problems that I referred to, still have the drive to do science, and they are going to continue to do science. What is very different is that in the last thirty years, science became a profession where many people could also do good science. I suspect this may have been an admirable and unusual era in the history of science. We're going back to a different kind of era where only a select few will actually do science.

FIELD: Institutional creativity is a profound problem. Being at both Harvard and the Smithsonian, I'm aware of conflicting requirements. The Smithsonian, among various government organizations, is probably more like a university than any other that I know. Nevertheless, there are requirements placed upon it of a bureaucratic nature. That's the way it is with federal funding. Harvard University should be holding high the concept of individual academic freedom to work on the projects that one wishes in an unfettered way. To a considerable extent I find that in our organization, which includes both Harvard and Smithsonian, there is a certain creative tension between the independent researchers within the faculty on the one hand, and the researchers on the staff of the Smithsonian federal establishment on the other hand. The organizations are not really the same thing; there's no sense pretending that they are. The constraints are different in the two organizations.

What is really troubling is that the president of Harvard University, President Bok, has expressed very great concern about the ability of the university to deal with government regulations.[5] He spends a great deal of his own time, personally, and has quite a large staff that does very little else but try and deal with government regulations. He feels that on the one hand government funding is critically needed and on the other hand it may ultimately seriously compromise academic freedom. It's a very serious problem that extends all across science. Other fields of learning have it as well. I do not know the answer.

HELLEGERS: Even in a Washington university like Georgetown, the president made exactly the same comment. However, I personally see the future for the individual who wants to go into science somewhat more rosily than perhaps you do, based on just straightforward obstetrical data. It is a fact that from ages ten to fifteen we have nineteen million children; from ages five to ten we have seventeen million; and from newly born to age five we have fifteen million. There will thus in fact be a 25 percent reduction in those trying to get into science. The fraction that gets there might very well remain the same. My suspicion is that there is a momentum in the field itself that obstetricians are not managing to keep up with. For the individual high school student here I'd say, "don't be depressed at all," the market may get very good.

TEMIN: As a faculty member in a state university, let me remind you that the legislators count up "full time equivalence," the buzz word at our university. Warm bodies who are attending classrooms decide the size of the faculty. Because of that, in the state of Wisconsin, tenured faculty, although not at the Madison campus and not necessarily the research faculty, were laid off. The past educational expansion since World War II has been primarily in the universities. This has been supported because there were more people to educate. The demographic data that we just heard mean fewer students, and legislators quite rightly are going to say fewer students should mean a smaller university budget. Eighty-five percent of the budget of higher education is for the personnel. When the 5-year-olds and below grow up, there will be something for them, but the question for the immediate graduates is not at all rosy for university faculty employment.

One solution suggested by Dr. David in a recent issue of *Science* was that there should be a new industry-university relationship.[6] This is a very encouraging kind of idea. He mentioned the Harvard-Monsanto contract as a model for the future. Perhaps this country has been so successful because of the pluralism of its institutions. Modes of financing will need something like industrial-university arrangements to tide us over and keep the vitality of academic science.

Participant: Dr. Temin, how did you get into virology? You never quite explained that. I am interested.

TEMIN: I happened to be at the Jackson Laboratory at Bar Harbor, Maine, in the early 1950s as a high school student. The Jackson Laboratory was built to produce and study in-bred mice, mice that are bred brother to sister so that they become genetically homogeneous. Such mice are used in cancer research and especially were used to prove that cancer was a genetic disease. Francisco Duran Reynolds, a Spanish virologist interested in the viral theory of cancer, came there one summer and gave our group of high school students one or two lectures. We also heard Ledwig Gross from the VA Hospital in Bronx, who had just discovered that a virus caused mouse leukemia, though the geneticists at the Jackson Laboratory proved that he was wrong. It turned out they were wrong in their proof! These lectures may have been a seed.

When I came to graduate school at the California Institute of Technology, I was interested in embryology and development. I spent my first year and a half working with development. When it was shown by people at Rutgers that adding a virus to cells would change them, I realized this was a form of development.[7] It was much easier to study development using a virus rather than the undetermined embryonically induced differentiators. From this interest in development I started to be a virologist. I have spent the last twenty-five years studying that ten-thousand-letter virus. There remains much more to study. I've become a virologist and, I guess, a molecular biologist, but still following that same change in cells.

HELLEGERS: Happenstance often does enable one to see a model that is more useful for doing something one is interested in. That is precisely what happened to me.

I took a degree in aviation medicine at the University of Paris. As a Dutchman I found no future in aviation medical labs because they were all closing down as a result of the secrecy of the work. A very nice physiologist in Paris suggested to me that the fetus *in utero* is really a high-altitude passenger, weightless, short of oxygen, and so forth. Realizing this, I did precisely what Dr. Field did. I started looking through a series of books, looked up who had been talking that way, and found that it had been an obstetrician in Baltimore, Dr. Nicholson J. Eastman.[8] He had been talking about notions of "Mount Everest *in utero*," meaning that the fetus in the womb is at the same height as you would be on top of Mount Everest. That thought switched me into obstetrics and fetal physiology. It was a nice model to play with and instead of having a lot of air force officers, I had a lot of good-looking young women to work with!

Participant: Is there any speculation about why there is a more complicated means of encoding the genetic message in vertebrates than in bacteria?

TEMIN: Yes, there's a lot of speculation. Biologists don't really have a theoretical biology, but there sure is a lot of speculative biology. It's thought that the present genes have been made up from primitive genes. If you take that whole message, as I had written, the ME was a little message. If you wanted to build up a big message, in traditional theory you have to duplicate that little message and then mutate it. For example, first would be ME ME, and then you would have ME MA. Then, perhaps, duplicate that and so build up a new, larger gene.

The speculation, which I find at least as interesting, is the idea that splitting genes is a very useful way to make up new genes. Go to the shelf, the previous genome, take the ME here and the MA here, and put them together. If one didn't work out, it is quite easy to recombine and change them to build up new combinations. The speculation is that this structure was selected as a way of handling genes, because it gave great ability to construct new and more complicated genes.

Alternatively, another explanation, which may be the same, is that the split gene structure gives a great deal more opportunity for control of gene function. In the case of a virus, you can control how much of the first message is processed to the second message, and how much of the second to the third. There is an enormous amount of beautiful work describing these control mechanisms.[9] You can see that there are whole other sets of control because you not only can control going from one message to another, but you can control the rearrangement of genes. There can be specificity in rearrangement. It may have been the existence of the ability to change the specificity of the rearrangement that was selected for this kind of structure.

What's very difficult in this kind of genetic evolution—and a lot of molecular biologists and virologists are very interested in evolution now—is that there are no fossils. We can test mechanisms of evolution in the laboratory in the sense of how things could change, but what we want to know about evolution is how things actually *did* change. There are no molecular fossils or anything, so it's not clear whether we'll be able to tell which of these reasons is correct. We can only determine what seems best to us, but what seems best to us may have nothing to do about actually why it is.

Participant: The sorts of things we have heard today show us that science is at a very difficult time. It's at a time when resources are being reduced. It's at a time when government regulations are increasing, and when it's difficult, particularly for young people, to decide about a possible career in science. As a scientist, I think it's extremely important for young people to know that science is very important for you to do for its own sake, per se. You should do what you want to do in that field because it is important to you.

This country has been engaged in the last several years with many, many social problems. These problems have been of primary importance, extreme importance, and progress has been made. There's much progress yet to be made. There are social problems, there are ecological problems, there are energy problems, and all that. The entire budget of the National Aeronautics and Space Administration, for instance, would keep the Department of Health and Human Services going for only eight days! It doesn't make much sense to throw all of that kind of resource into solving those other problems.

The future lies with those who take it and make it happen. Don't let these inequities discourage you, and don't necessarily do things because they look as though they will be only useful. Do them because they're important. I think that's an important message we should get across.

HELLEGERS: I think it's also been gotten across that science is good fun and that's helpful!

"On First Hearing": The Act of Creation in Music

WILLIAM SCHUMAN

One of the most distinguished musical personalities of this country; president emeritus of the Juilliard School and of the Lincoln Center for the Performing Arts. Honors include the first Pulitzer Prize in Music, the first New York Music Critics' Circle Award, two Guggenheim Fellowships, an award from the National Institute of Arts and Letters, the Gold Medal of Honor from the National Arts Club, and more than twenty honorary degrees. Strongly influenced by his former Juilliard teacher Roy Harris, and by his own intimate acquaintance with the rhythms of jazz and popular music.

Schuman's compositions are considered to be among the most "American" to be heard today. He has written ten symphonies and many other orchestral, choral, and chamber works.

COMMENT BY WALTER SHROPSHIRE, JR.
[At the colloquium, a concert followed these remarks.]

"Creativity is often the ability to see new relationships among familiar objects and structures. All researchers build upon the past. What is so startling is when someone sees a different way of connecting ideas that opens up whole new avenues of thought. In fact, established laws suddenly stand naked in their revealed incompleteness.

"Creativity in music is thus the same as in the sciences. A composer takes a familiar twelve-toned octave and, by arranging these tones in different patterns of dynamics, rhythmic duration, and sequence, produces new music that both startles and delights in its originality.

Figure 35. Einstein enjoyed playing the violin.

"In celebrating the creativity of Einstein, we are fascinated to learn about the forces and personal experiences that fuel such creative imaginations. Our curiosity drives us to search out clues that might also assist us to be more creative. For each of us has an inward yearning and suspicion that we, too, possess an imaginative potential that unfortunately, for many reasons, goes largely untapped throughout our lives. Perhaps, by the exercise of this curiosity we will prime the pump of our own genius."

I have looked forward to this event for many, many weeks now. I'm sure that all of you by now are sated with stories about Albert Einstein, some of them genuine, some of them apocryphal. I'll give you one that I can guarantee you have not heard before—and that is true. Many years ago, when I was at the Juilliard School, our string quartet was invited to go down to Princeton to play with Albert Einstein. The next day Robert Mann, the first violinist of the Juilliard Quartet, called me. I said, "Well, how was it Bobby?" "Oh, it was a marvelous evening. It was wonderful to be there, to be with such a great man, but musically there was a great problem." I said, "What was that?" He said, "the man can't count!"

I'm going to extemporize about what I think "On First Hearing" means to a composer. Before I get to that, I want to give you a quotation I like by the biochemist Szent-Györgyi.[1]

> Scientific thinking means that if we are faced with a problem, we approach it without preconceived ideas and sentiments like fear, greed, and hatred. We approach it with a cool head and collect data which we eventually try to fit together. This is all there is to it. It may sound simple and easy. What makes it difficult is the fact that our brain is not made to search for truth. It is but another organ of survival like fangs or claws, so the brain does not search for truth, but for advantage. It tries to make us accept this truth, what is only self-interest, allowing our thoughts to be dominated by our desires.

Now a great scientist could make such a disclaimer. It certainly makes my position as a man of the arts much easier, because obviously I'm supposed to be the emotional type and you the intellectual types. Of course, there is no difference we know of in the creative process. Emotions and intellectual capacity are naturally intertwined. Both exist as science and art.

In musical composition, research is the ordering of the properties of sound into special juxtapositions, which we call "personal profile" or "style." The mark of a major composer is that his statement is unique. Only that particular composer could create those "data." The materials into which sound is organized are present for all, much as scientific data are broadly available. It is the special insight of the composer that goes beyond the perceived limitations. That is the creative element, be it in art or in science.

Let us now consider "On First Hearing." I want to give you briefly some idea of what it means to be a composer and to be in an audience, hearing a work of his for the first time. I'm sixty-eight years old, I've been through this three hundred, maybe four hundred times. Each time it's the same. It's like having a tooth pulled. If you go to a baseball game, you are in the midst of a gang, an audience, fans, who really understand the game. They understand it much more than just seeing that the pitcher is throwing balls over the plate, that the catcher's receiving them, or the batter is occasionally hitting one and someone is running. They observe these facts. But in addition, they observe the counterpoint of the game. They observe that the outfield shifts for certain players. They observe a thousand subtleties that take place all at once.

The problem with a piece of new music is that it lacks familiarity. In music, familiarity does not breed contempt, rather it breeds understanding and love, and familiarity is probably 80 percent of the joy of music. If you hear a new piece, the composer knows—if he's sensitive, and heaven knows I'm sensitive—that his audience is missing 80 percent of the joy, just by definition. Furthermore, when you come into the hall, and the piece starts, people begin to whisper, or they don't pay attention. The first desire the composer has is to borrow your ears for the length of time that the piece takes. Mostly, people don't pay attention. They don't pay attention to anything really, not just music, but especially music.

I referred previously to the similarities of data in science and the creative process in the arts. These are true, but what is enormously different is the evaluative process. When a scientific discovery is completed—I know it doesn't take place all at once and I know that much of the work on it has been going on for years—but once the product is announced, the scientific community doesn't have to understand it in twenty-five minutes, as you will my piece tonight. Scientists read it at their leisure, they discuss it, and they can consider it for years. But when a new piece of music is played, that 20 percent content I said was available to you, that 20 percent, or the entire work, if you choose, must make some mark. If it doesn't, it will never be heard again—or is likely never to be heard again.

That's what's so strange. This is what the composer is up against: the propositions (a) no one really wants to *hear* a new piece and (b) one doesn't have much chance of enjoying it because it's all so strange. You might ask, "how does a composer survive?" I survive because there are always a few people who like it. Sometimes they are my colleagues and my family—which is of course obliged to! There are always enough people to respond to it, and so, little by little, the piece worms its way into the repertoire and that's very nice.

When I was invited to participate in this colloquium I was asked if I would do an evening of my music. I wanted to play safe, so I opened it with a piece I knew you would like by a great composer [Bach], and then I thought I would project my latest composition. Notice I didn't call it my last, as someone said. It is, I hope, my *latest*!

Let me tell you what some of the listening problems are and just for fun together, paint broad brush strokes without giving you a music appreciation lesson. This audience is very disciplined, because there was no applause between any of the movements of the Bach. The soloist [Donald McInnes, violist] gave you every opportunity because he had all those nice long pauses. That was impressive. Academics aren't wrong all the time, you see.

In the first place, someone has asked me before what a "setting" was. Is it a visual setting? In this case it's not visual. This is a poem from Shakespeare's Henry the Eighth. It is a poem that was set to music by me many, many years ago.[2] I wanted to base this work on that song. You might ask why I chose this particular combination of sounds. The question is one that I can't answer precisely because I do not know what process led me to that choice. I only know that it was the right choice for the kinds of things I was thinking about, perhaps not entirely consciously. As an amusing thing, let me give you some idea of what's going to take place, and see how much you can follow. If you can't follow it, don't let me know, just yell "Bravo" at the end and everything will be all right!

The piece starts with a simple chord on the harp, and the singer announces a little anticipatory variation on what's going to come later. The alto flute intones this melody and then you'll hear—I'm not going to describe this piece blow by blow, so don't get nervous, because that would take longer than the piece—various filigree effects coming in, with the viola commenting upon it and the other instruments coming upon it. It proceeds this way to develop the melody, which you have not yet heard sung but which will be reiterated several times with increasingly intriguing and beautiful contrapuntal effects. Right?

All this leads in due course to a fast section, and here you are really going to have to work very hard because you're not going to be able to hear it all at once. I'm not being funny. One of the conceits very often is—it's usually not a lay listener's, especially a sophisticated lay listener's—that you think you can hear a piece the first time. No professional would make that claim—unless he is a critic! It is virtually impossible to hear everything that goes on the first time. The work must be heard many, many times. Of course, unless a work supplies the desire for repeated hearings, it's not really a work of art. It's all over at one sitting, at one listening.

Next is a fast section. The voice during this entire middle fast section is used as an instrument of the ensemble. The sounds that she sings are syllables. They are phonetics, and they are not random phonetics. They are phonetics that I have written out to describe the qualities of the music that is being played. It's sort of an up-to-date scat, somebody told me. I started using them when I was seventeen years old. Using the phonetics, you'll hear the voice as part of the ensemble. The ensemble will go through all sorts of gyrations, all related to the tune. Sometimes you'll recognize it more often. I suppose on the first hearing you may not, that isn't important.

I hope you get the idea of a long, languid introduction going into the fast

Figure 36. Holographic page of "In Sweet Music" by William Schuman.

section, building up to a climax, and a very quiet section before the melody returns. Eventually it returns and then the singer rises and sings the song, "Orpheus with His Lute." This time there are new contrapuntal embellishments and the piece comes to a very quiet and serene close. Thank you for the opportunity of giving you these few words of warning.

[The audience listened to the work. At the conclusion, following extended applause, William Schuman went to the center of the stage and answered questions from the audience.]

SCHUMAN: The program calls for discussion, and if you have any questions that you would like to address to the performers, or to me, or any comments that are kind, we'd be happy to hear from you. How did you make out, all of you, in listening? [Extensive applause]

Participant: Were you thinking of any particular images when you wrote the music?

SCHUMAN: I'm always thinking of a double bar when I'm writing music. That's not a joke, that's the end. Not to be facetious, images, no. When I'm writing music I think of the music and the properties of the music. Only in music appreciation courses do they talk about images. Writing music is a hard pursuit and you have to pay attention to it. You have no time for images. At least I don't.

Participant: What limitations in the performers inform your writing of the music, for example, the voice? Were there times when the voice said, "I just can't do that, or voices can't do that?"

SCHUMAN: Actually, one of the wonderful things about writing chamber music is that you have an opportunity to work so closely with performers. You have a chance to change things if you want to change. They are usually editorial changes, because if you've been at any profession, including writing music for as many years as I have, it doesn't necessarily mean that you get better, but at least you know what you're doing. In the early days, I remember writing ballet scores. You'd only have one general rehearsal with the dancers and the orchestra before the performance. You'd have one general rehearsal that day, or the day before, and everything had better be in place. When you write an extended work for a soloist, the situation is different, and I wrote such a work for Don McInnes. He's recorded it with Bernstein and the Philharmonic. It was Concerto on Old English Rounds and I'd never written for solo viola before. Don said, "Well, just write anything that comes into your head. Write anything you want. We can always tame it." When you work with a musician of his capabilities, that's a wonderful experience to have because he would say, "I know what you're getting at. I think the writing may be a little too thick." Then he'd play it for me and I might change it. So you had a special thing. If you write for great performers, you have an opportunity of working with them instead of when you write more routinely for large orchestras and things of that kind. Of course, you don't often have that opportunity, but I think the thought behind this question is an excellent one. The players do inform in that sense, in every meaning of that sense. I'm not an experimental composer. I don't try to extend. I have no need to try and extend the capabilities of the performers, although some of them claim that I do.

Participant: How long did it take you to write the serenade and how did you sustain the mood necessary to do so during that length of time?

SCHUMAN: There are two questions. I imagine I took the better part of the year to write it and I certainly didn't sustain that mood during that entire year. If I had I would not be here with my wife this evening, I can tell you that. I think there's an enormous difference between going into your study each morning and taking up from where you left off. At the end of the morning you throw away a lot of it and keep some of it.

As for the mood, I presume that most of you would say that you go to your desk and you do your work, and then comes a lunch break. You have lunch with a colleague and you know you can't carry on that mood. In other words, the personal mood for a year—that would be impossible but whenever you get back to the work that mood is there. Although I never really think of the mood. It's a strange thing. You're doing your work. Although I like the use of the word "mood," because to me, it means sort of an overall ambience. That's really what I work in. What is the emotional climate of the music that I'm writing? That to me is the most important part and I think that's perhaps what you had in mind.

Participant: When you, as composer, hear the work performed, for a second or third time, are there any new insights that come to you?

SCHUMAN: Let me answer historically in terms of a life of work. I hear some pieces that I wish I'd never published. I hear others where there are some pages that I think could be better. I hear others that I absolutely love. I find that the further away in time I get from a piece, the more objective I become. There is a concerto of mine, a piano concerto, that was just recently recorded.[3] I wrote it when I was twenty-five and I used to be very brash in those days. I had the things published even before I ever heard them; I was so sure. Now my publisher goes crazy because I want this in my studio for six months before I give it to him to put into print. But that early piano concerto, I didn't like. I was twenty-seven, twenty-eight, or thirty years old. For years I didn't like it. Two years ago a young pianist told me that he was playing it. He restored my faith in it, and I knew when it happened. While I was very young, I was sort of disdainful of it because I was going on to other things. Now that I'm no longer young, I see that I did things then that I could never do now. I'm aware of the enormous differences. I'm sure this isn't true of the greatest creators in the world, but it is certainly true of me. There are enormous differences at different times of one's life. I could never have written this present piece in my twenties or thirties, never. I wouldn't have been able to do that because it's only as you get older that you can reveal more of your emotions. Young people are up-tight more, I think. When you are very young you can do a lot of useful things that are very vigorous and very athletic, that you really can't later. At least I don't think you can. I'm not speaking personally, I'm really speaking about the literature of music as I observe it. I think that profound statements, emotional statements, tend to come later on rather than earlier. The earlier things have a quality, of course, that's absolutely delicious. That you don't capture again.

Participant: Did you benefit from the criticism by music critics of your works, in writing better ones?

SCHUMAN: Better things, only in the sense that I learned how to control my temper. Seriously, though, when we speak of criticism, we tend to think of criticism only in terms of journalism. Of course, there are some marvelous people writing for newspapers, and there are some people who aren't well equipped to do so. It just depends on what town you're in. I almost know before a piece is played what kind of a notice I will get. Washington, D.C., I should say, is a town in which I usually bat 500, which isn't bad.

Participant: I was wondering whether any of your performers felt particularly preferred or neglected by the music?

SCHUMAN: That's a very good question. Don, why don't you answer it?

Donald McInnes: We all know our parts. We all know the piece, obviously. You always hear that at a performance. I think in this case, getting a little more down to your question, one of the characteristics of a great composer, I believe, is where a performer can relate to the writer. With William Schuman, there's no problem among performers. One of the reasons for this is simply because he makes it his duty to know the capabilities of an instrument before he writes for it. Therefore, the instrumentalist feels at home with the music, and this isn't always the case.

SCHUMAN: I should leave when the audience asks the wrong questions.

Participant: I've always been fascinated by just the art of composing itself. I wonder if there's any way of explaining how, in the act of composing, the music falls to different parts. Do you hear this as something you are trying to express, or what is this lovely procedure, whereby you get an idea and it ends up on paper and is distributed among the instruments of an ensemble or orchestra?

SCHUMAN: I was present once when Virgil Thomson [American composer and critic] was asked that question. He said it would cost you $50 an hour.
It's a wonderful question, but a very tough one to answer. You might ask a painter how he chooses a paint and how he mixes all his hues. The art of composition—I don't mean to sound pretentious—but among other things,

it's an intellectual pursuit that relates to what we were saying earlier in the evening. Before you can even be a bad composer, you have to study for twelve years, because there are technical things that have to be done. Once you have the technical mastery, the technical know-how, of course, has nothing to do with what you say or whether it may be worth saying or not. However, the choice of how you are saying it is part of what you're saying. In other words, if I write successfully, I couldn't have written the harp part for a piano. It would have been impossible, because the harp is exactly the sound required. It's not just the sound, it's the medium through which you wish to say what you're going to say.

It's impossible for me to give you an answer in words. If I could give you an answer in words, there would be no place for music. It's its own language. A young student might ask, "why did you write this for an oboe, or did you just write something and assign it to an oboe?" That doesn't happen. A mature composer usually hears it altogether. That doesn't mean that he might not make a sketch of an orchestra to follow, but it's all part of the same process. You don't write something and then choose the instrument. I didn't answer that very well, but it's too difficult to do. Maybe someday I can answer it better. I'm aware that I didn't, but I love the question.

Participant: It's often been said that there's a relationship between the performers and the audience. I wonder if the performers can share with us how they felt that relationship was this evening.

SCHUMAN: That's a very interesting question. I think we should first ask if there are any critics here.

Flutist, Sue Ann Kahn: One can tell, one has some feeling back from the audience. There's no question about it. One of the things that one senses is the way an audience listens. If there's a certain kind of silence, I think. I sensed tonight that attention was very much on the music, and we certainly had ours there. We shared that attention together with the audience. I don't know if my colleagues feel the same, but I certainly did feel a very deep concentration by the audience and appreciation.

SCHUMAN: I certainly felt that too, and I thought they might have been frightened not to after my opening remarks.

Participant: Would it have made any difference if there were a critic here?

SCHUMAN: I presume that there are critics present. I hope there are.

Participant: Do you ever structure a program so that a new piece of work will be played twice in one evening?

SCHUMAN: Maybe we could do this work again, if you like. At the Lincoln Center the Chamber Music Society subscribers have suggested that we always put the new pieces last, so if they are concerned about the late hour, they could leave and go back to the suburbs before the performance. In the early days we used to repeat pieces at the end. But, of course, for a long work, besides the fatigue of the performers, it's too much to hear twice. Come back tomorrow and we'll do it again. It's a lovely idea to hear it again.

Participant: Does it happen with any frequency nowadays that a young composer succeeds without having gone through studies at one of our great music schools?

SCHUMAN: That's an interesting question. There are many composers who have not gone through one of our great music schools. There are a lot of very fine composers teaching in colleges, and I suppose there are some composers who are successful who were in the beginning self-taught. To answer your question, I don't know if there are any, I presume there are. Not every successful young composer today has gone to a music school, but if he goes to a university, it's the same thing. He gets the same kind of instruction.

It's an easier question about whether a composer can be self-taught. There are some composers who have been self-taught, but I don't know any composer in the history of music who didn't study the music of other composers. It's as though science were suddenly starting today, as though there weren't anything before. We have our heritage and the heritage is all the music that we know from the beginning of time. All that we've discovered so far. I think mostly, of course, composers do study formally. It's like asking a singer or instrumentalist whether they learn without going to a school or without going to a master. Rarely it happens. I suppose it could. I know of no instances.

Participant: I'm hearing you talk about the acceptance of your piece and the audience. I was thinking of an interesting contrast between scientists and composers. The scientists, through the processes of professional societies, have been able to insulate themselves increasingly from popular audiences, and listen more and more to their peers. Do you envy the scientists?

SCHUMAN: I want to tell you that music is accused of doing the same thing. It's absolutely true that there are many societies that are devoted to the playing of new music. There are some composers, some honored colleagues, who feel that the advanced techniques today require this. For example, the technique of say Pierre Boulez, who has a great institute in Paris for study and research in acoustical phenomena, basically in composition.[4] Many feel that today's composers need such specialized audiences of their peers. I happen not to be one, although I think the other is very valuable and comes more under the line of research.

Within music there have always been certain composers who are "experimental." Charles Ives was not subconsciously an experimental composer, but Henry Cowell, for example, has been, or John Cage, or any number of others that one could mention who are consciously experimental composers.

It doesn't make them better composers or poorer composers. It's merely a descriptive phrase I'm using, because in my judgment, I'm a romantic. The greatest thing that can happen to you as a composer is that something you wrote enters the stream of music, which is a long and noble and marvelous stream. It's all traditional. Everything that I know has always been built on something out of the past, just as I believe—heaven knows, it's a dangerous thing for me to say before a scientific audience—that every technology that I've read about is always built on a previous technology. I think that's generally true. Maybe there are exceptions. It certainly is true in music that the techniques go that way.

Participant: I'm wondering as you go about your work, how do you go about setting your priorities as far as what types of music you compose? How do you choose one as the highest priority?

SCHUMAN: I accept commissions, and I've written only on commission since I was very, very young. I choose the commissions that I want to do. People ask for the pieces. Somebody asks me for a chamber music work, and if I want to write a symphony, I don't accept that commission. The priority to me is the work that I want to write at that time. I'm always thinking ahead a couple of years as to what I should write. Is that what you meant?

Participant: To what extent do you start with a complete idea of what you want in a piece beforehand, as opposed to starting and seeing where perhaps it leads you?

SCHUMAN: I do a little of each. I'm working now on a work for French horn for the New York Philharmonic.[5] I know it's going to be performed, God willing, next January. I'm not terribly far into it, but I do have some ideas. For the first time in my life I've written it out of sequence. I've written the two outer movements because they are both slow movements. I haven't written the middle one because it's too difficult, and everytime I think of it, I don't have any ideas. Then the other day I heard a horn work by a colleague, Dr. Schuller.[6] It is so marvelous, I don't know why anyone else would ever want to write for the horn. That's going to set me back another two weeks. Generally speaking, you just work at it. You really just work at it, the same as anybody else. Any system works except neglect. It's work.

Participant: Speaking only for myself, I felt kind of a thrill as the door opened and your performers came in garbed, as they were, in a kind of classical dress. There's a kind of courtesy that pertains between performers and audience, that has something to do with formal dress. Is there a kind of code to be followed?

Harpist, Susan Jolles: There definitely is. There was a time, I guess in the early seventies, when musicians were experimenting with having very casual dress on stage. Women came out in pants, men wore black turtlenecks, and tails were a thing of the past. We felt that it wasn't respectful to the audience in a sense. It also didn't create the right atmosphere for music, and we do like to dress in a presentable way that makes the audience feel that it's part of the program.

Participant: In your work do you quote or allude to yourself or other composers?

SCHUMAN: I certainly hope I don't quote other composers.

Participant: But you said this piece is based on an earlier work.

SCHUMAN: Yes. This is based on a song that I wrote many years ago. I'm very fond of this song. I love it. Speaking of things that you like that you wrote, I absolutely love this song. Someday I'm going to do another piece on it. I was so happy about it. One of my colleagues came to me after the first performance and said, "It's a marvelous piece, why did you use an old English song?" He couldn't believe that I wrote it. The point is, no, I do not consciously use quotes. This particular work is based on this song.

Participant: You mentioned a few moments ago that through the music you were trying to say something that can't be said in words. Can you say anything about what you were trying to say?

SCHUMAN: No, it's impossible to do that. I'm not saying that people can't try to describe music in words. People do it all the time, but it doesn't get you very far. If I were to describe this music to you in words, I would have to tell you something like the following: The work opens. The alto flute answers, starts on the note of D, holds it three slow beats, after which there is a descending minor second. I mean, I could describe it all to you in technical terms. That's the only thing you can do in words.

Participant: I didn't mean for you to describe what the music was. I meant describe what you are trying to say in music.

SCHUMAN: What I was trying to say is what you heard.

Participant: In terms of creativity, are there advantages and disadvantages to writing in a particular style; in other words, making music that can readily be identified by being of a particular control unit?

SCHUMAN: I don't think a composer has that choice unless he's a commercial composer. Starting out to win a wide audience is a perfectly honorable thing to do as long as you know what you're doing. It seems to me that the composers of serious music write the best music that they can. Some of it is popular and some of it isn't popular.

Participant: You hear music and you can say that sounds like Brahms, or you hear music and say that sounds like Mozart. These different pieces sound similar in quality and therefore mark the identity as being from the same composer.

SCHUMAN: That's right. That process is going on today as it always has gone on. There are more recent composers than those you cited. All you're saying in effect is that when the style becomes particularly well known, it's recognizable as such. This is what is known as personal profile or style.

Participant: Style is one thing. It is neither a good thing nor a bad thing.

SCHUMAN: It's a fact. I mean, I think it's a good thing, because it's the thing that makes the composer special. You recognize his style.

Participant: If you could pick your second hearing in any audience in any city, where would you pick?

SCHUMAN: Right here, this same audience.

Participant: Why did you pick this particular piece for this particular occasion?

SCHUMAN: Because it's my latest piece. I'm still in love with it and I thought it was a nice thing to do here tonight. Everything about it. I wanted to do chamber music and I thought I was terribly modest by not doing a whole evening of my music as I was asked to do. But we soon forgot the Bach. I mean, you've heard that before!

Participant: About creativity. Do you yourself feel this is one of your more creative pieces?

SCHUMAN: Every piece I write is creative. Some of them are less successful than others. When you say creative, "you make it up." I'm using creative as a descriptive and not a qualitative term. You make it up. It's creative. I made up a story.

Participant: I'm interested in the origin of ideas and form. One of the analyses often given for the arts and new ideas is analogy from structure. Can you say anything about where form and shape fit in and whether analogy is playing a role?

SCHUMAN: I can't. I mean, it's not that I'm unwilling, but I don't know how to answer your question. I honestly don't. I'm not trying to be funny. I just don't know.

Participant: It just comes?

SCHUMAN: No, nothing just comes. It comes from hard work. But it's not a conscious thing of saying: what was the analogy; why does this happen? You write it; you sit at your desk and you work. You invent melody, you invent countermelodies, you invent rhythms, you invent orchestral colors, you invent textures, and you invent things that you want to do. It's a creative process and I know I'm being a terrible bore by saying after the twelfth time that I can't describe in words what the process is. Believe me, I wish I could. The next time I lecture here, I'm going to think up some answer. Honestly, I don't know. I feel frustrated that I can't answer that.

Participant: When Picasso was asked a similar question, he said, "Well, if I had wanted to use words, I would have written a book."

SCHUMAN: When Picasso said that, there was also a woman who looked at his paintings and kept saying, "What is that?" He said, "That's a chair."

"That's a chair?," she said.

"You see it there? That's the way I see it," he said. "And you see there? That's a face."

"That's a face?"

"Yes, that's the way I see it."

She said, "Well, tell me. If your eyesight is so poor why do you paint?"

Thanks very much.

Biomedical Investigation

ROSALYN S. YALOW

Senior Medical Investigator and Chief, Nuclear Medicine, Veterans Administration Hospital, Bronx, New York; research professor and Distinguished Service Professor, Mount Sinai School of Medicine; editorial board, *Diabetes*, and coeditor, *Hormone and Metabolic Research*; member, National Academy of Sciences; winner of Nobel Prize for Physiology or Medicine, 1977.

"Perhaps the earliest memories I have are of being a stubborn, determined child. Through the years my mother has told me that it was fortunate that I chose to do acceptable things, for if I had chosen otherwise no one could have deflected me from my path. . . . By seventh grade I was committed to mathematics. A great [high school] . . . teacher . . . excited my interest in chemistry, but when I went to [Hunter College], my interest was diverted to physics. . . . In the late '30's . . . physics, and in particular nuclear physics, was the most exciting field in the world. . . . I was excited about achieving a career in physics. My family, being more practical, thought the most desirable position for me would be as an elementary school teacher. Furthermore, it seemed most unlikely that good graduate schools would accept and offer financial support for a woman in physics. However, my physics professors encouraged me and I persisted. . . .

"Through the years . . . I . . . have enjoyed the time spent with the 'professional children,' the young investigators who trained in our laboratory and who are now scattered throughout the world. . . . In the training in my laboratory the emphasis has been not only on learning our research techniques but also our philosophy. I have never aspired to have, nor do I now want, a laboratory or a cadre of investigators-in-training which is more extensive than I can personally interact with and supervise. . . ."

When I heard Professors Singer and Field, I had a sinking feeling that I was at the wrong centennial. I recognized from the things they said, and what I knew about Einstein, that if this is what it means to be a scientist, I couldn't compete in this area at all.

My approach to science is not to see the world in its totality and then try and bring reason into it. I belong, perhaps, at the Marie Curie centennial, because my approach to science very much resembles hers. The development of an idea, the performing of a few feasibility studies, and then having the endurance and capacity to see the idea through to the end.

In my discussion of this with Professor Field, he commented that perhaps I felt more in tune with Marie Curie because she was a physicist—and a woman. I answered very quickly that I would have felt just as at ease in speaking at Rutherford's centennial[1] because the spirit that he developed in Cavendish, the feeling that you would discuss a problem at lunch, would go into the laboratory and within a day or a week you would define an answer, this was my kind of science. This is why I have worked in what I like to call small science. You define a problem, you see an experiment, you learn from the experiment, and you generate a new problem.

I was relieved, however, and thought that perhaps I did have a role in this centennial celebration when it became evident that what we are talking about here is not even the joys of scientific research, but the joys of creativity. When I heard Mr. Schuman's remarks, I recognized that in the diversity of our fields, we all have so much in common in the way in which we interact in new ideas with our perceptions of our roles. I would like to return now to my role as a scientist.

One of the students asked, "How do we make our way in research?" On reflection, I thought that for most of us, this is not really a meaningful question at the student stage. There are Mozarts and Einsteins who make their way in a manner that most of the rest of us cannot understand. But for most of us who do make our way in research, at the teenage level, the college level, and even at the graduate school level, we have probably decided on science or history or art or music. At this stage, however, very infrequently do we have an appreciation that we will be creative. There are many scientists. A small fraction of these really do research in the sense of uncovering new and unpredictable bits of information. Among those who do research, very few are really original, innovative, and change our concepts of the world around us. Most of us are satisfied with a lesser course. How do we choose which route we will take? I wandered into science, perhaps, by avoiding the things I cannot do. I could not have chosen music as a career; I'm tone deaf. I have absolutely no artistic talent. I am probably the world's worst athlete. This left a few intellectual occupations, and at an early age I began to think in terms of mathematics or history. Mathematics appealed more to my personality at a stage when it was only arithmetic. Where I went in science depended on where I was, what my teachers were like, and what science at that time was doing. In junior high school, I knew it was arithmetic, algebra, and even a little bit of geometry. In high school, I soon found a chemistry teacher who taught me the joys of working with my hands along with my mind. In high school, there was no doubt I was going to be a chemistry major.

I entered Hunter College, which in those days was a woman's college. The chemistry department was very large. Chemistry was taught by mass production in relatively large courses, and there was no teacher who really cared about me as an individual. We had a very small physics department. Because this was the Great Depression and jobs were scarce, Hunter had a very distinguished physics department in the 1930s, compared to what one might have expected in a woman's college. We had Professor Jerrold Zacharias,[2] who subsequently went to the Massachusetts Institute of Technology. We had Professor Duane Roller,[3] who edited the *American Journal of Physics* and was an author of the textbook from which we studied; Robert A. Millikan; and Ernest C. Watson.[4] We had Professor Herbert Otis, who was not very distinguished as a physicist and is certainly unknown to the physicists among you. However, from the very beginning, he made sure that I did a lot of extra work, a lot of extra reading, and in addition, gave me the opportunity to develop new experiments in the laboratory. These were not research, but experiments that could be used in a college physics laboratory. For me, these were new and innovative. These three people generated the kinds of interest in science that became my own.

They did have a little bit of help. The period of the thirties was certainly the greatest time of innovation in the fields of radioactivity and nuclear physics, which became my fields of interest. There was also Eve Curie's biography of her mother, who became a role model after I knew the kinds of things I wanted.[5] There was also some trouble. It wasn't easy for a woman in physics in the 1930s, when even men were not getting jobs. However, I switched to a physics major in my senior year.

I thought I was going to apply for graduate work in physics. Professor Zacharias thought I should have a backup. His wife, a biochemist, worked with Professor Rudolf Schoenheimer, probably one of the country's leading biochemists.[6] Professor Zacharias suggested that in my senior year it would be well if I took a job as a secretary in Schoenheimer's laboratory. In this way, I could be exposed to the great, could earn my way, and take a few graduate courses on the side. I had had the wisdom when I entered college to take typing. Not only that, but I had studied German, and could read Professor Schoenheimer's Germanic handwriting. I had had a little bit of experience in the laboratory, so I could make his slides as well. Therefore, I appeared to be a very useful secretary! The only thing left was to take stenography, which I agreed to do when I graduated in January 1941, magna cum laude, Junior Phi Beta Kappa, and prepared to be a secretary so I could get into science via the back door.

It turned out that it was good fortune that Duane Roller was a well-known leader in educational physics. He had friends throughout the country. He embarked on a campaign to get me into graduate school. He did receive one letter back that said, "She's a Jew and a woman, and we can never get her a job afterwards. If you would guarantee to get her a job, then we would take her into our graduate school."

I recognized this was neither anti-Semitism nor antifeminism. This was a realistic attitude, for in the 1930s one simply could not get a job for a Jewish woman in physics. Roller said, "Don't worry." He would get me a job afterwards. I would have been offered that fellowship, but I had the good fortune that it was September of 1941. Men with my qualifications were being drafted, and the University of Illinois did take me in as the first woman they'd accepted with a graduate assistantship in physics in the College of Engineering since 1917. There are certain similarities between 1917 and 1941! I don't know why one was surprised by Pearl Harbor.

The first semester in graduate school was not easy. Apart from meeting my husband, it really was a tough time. I had come from a woman's college. I had not been a physics major until my upper senior year, because that was the first time Hunter College had offered the physics major. As an upper senior, I took enough physics to complete the major. I think I had nine or twelve credits of physics as an upper senior, some of which, such as thermodynamics, were not given at Hunter.

I had to go to City College in New York and take it at night. When I got into graduate school, I realized that having come from a woman's college, I did not have the same physics background as did the men who entered when I did. Therefore, I sat in on two undergraduate courses, was a graduate assistant, taught eight hours a week, and took three graduate courses. Not only that, but as a graduate assistant I was a little bit insecure. I had never taught physics before. Physics instruction at Hunter, where we had relatively small classes and a senior professor, was very different from physics instruction at the University of Illinois, where there was a major lecture given by a senior professor and recitation sections run by graduate assistants. Therefore, in addition to everything else, I sat in on the recitation section of one of the young instructors, who was considered one of the best teachers of the year. This kept me relatively busy! At the end of the first semester, I got A's in two of the graduate courses, an A in optics lecture and an A minus in the optics laboratory. The sole comment of the acting head of the department as he looked at my grades was to say, "That A minus shows that women really don't do well in laboratory work." Despite his pessimism and a really hard schedule, I received my Ph.D. three and one-half years after I entered.

These were the war years; we were teaching the soldiers and the sailors who were being sent back to the universities. Our own staff was being decimated, largely by the Manhattan Project. I practically cried when they took away the last 100-microamp meter to Los Alamos. When I did graduate, however, I felt I had justified myself and it was easier for the University of Illinois Physics Department to accept women in the future.

I returned to New York as the first woman engineer at the ITT Research Laboratories, in a very bright unit consisting of theoretical physicists and mathematicians. At the end of the war some months later, this unit collapsed when the Jewish-French engineers returned to France.

A number of the physicists returned to other positions. J.B.H. Kuper, who had been Chief of the Division, went to Brookhaven National Laboratories as head of health physics and instrumentation. I went back to Hunter to teach. Fifteen hours of teaching a week was not quite enough for me and Hunter had no research facilities at the time. I looked for something else to do. Through my husband, who had already gone into medical physics, I met Dr. Edith Quimby, who was the leading woman medical physicist in the country. She took me to see Dr. G. Failla, who was certainly the dean of the medical physicists in the country. He spoke to me for fifteen minutes and made a phone call. I heard him say, "Bernie,[7] if you want to get radioisotopes, there's somebody you must hire." I had my job at the Bronx Veterans Administration Hospital. Although I never had a course in biology in my life, my work was to be the application of radioisotopes in medicine.

It was necessary to be an engineer in those days. We simply did not have equipment. If you come to my laboratory even now, we have a museum of the power supplies that I built because I had been an electrical engineer. We have the bismuth-walled Geiger counters, which were designed according to my specifications because we needed higher sensitivity for the detection of gamma rays than silver-walled Geiger counters have. We had problems even in calibration of isotopes. We sent patients with radioiodine in their thyroids around to the various New York hospitals to establish the "New York millicurie" for Iodine-131. I don't feel so old, yet this was the state of the art at that time.

Certainly one who was trained in physics was absolutely essential to get medical applications of isotopes off the ground when isotopes were released from Oak Ridge in 1947. I pay tribute to the Veterans Administration because it recognized that the use of radioisotopes in medicine was a combined clinical and research function. We had to develop the modalities if we were going to use them at all. In 1947 radioisotope services were established in seven of the VA hospitals as joint research-clinical programs. From this, the medical specialty of nuclear medicine developed.

When I came in, it certainly was thought that radioisotopes should be used principally for the treatment of cancer. We were using radioiodine to treat thyroid cancer and we were using Phosphorus-32 for the treatment of leukemia and polycythemia. I read Hevesy's book *Radioactive Indicators*.[8] It was absolutely clear to me that treatment of cancer wasn't where the future of radioisotopes in medicine was. The future lay in understanding physiology. For those physicists who tend to go into nuclear medicine and related enterprises, it would be a good idea to reread *Radioactive Indicators* in order to appreciate how much was known, before we had reactors, in terms of the applicability of radioisotopes in medicine. Recognizing the way in which applications were going to go, I felt that we needed an internist. Since I was in the Department of Radiotherapy, I went to our chief of medicine and said, "You know we'll take anybody whom you think will work out well in our program." He replied, "I have a resident, the smartest resident I've ever had. He has another job, but if you can talk him into coming, it would be great for you and great for science." Solomon Berson[9] joined our service as internist, four years later he became its chief, and with him over a twenty-two year period I learned enough medicine for the work we did. We worked as very close collaborators, physician and physicist. I think he probably wanted to be a physicist. I wanted to be a physician. He was certainly very skilled in math and physics. We learned to talk each other's language and think each other's ideas. It was a very fruitful collaboration until his death in 1972.

What were some of the problems we worked on initially? The first applications were in the use of Iodine 131 to gain an appreciation of thyroid physiology; the mechanisms of the thyroidal uptake of iodine followed by its conversion to the organically bound form, then its subsequent release and degradation. We also made use of Hevesy's isotope dilution principle in order to study body compartmental size. We used the method first to measure the blood by injecting radiolabeled red cells or serum proteins and sampling at ten to twenty minutes. Subsequently, we appreciated that following intravenous administration of radioactive sodium, it will eventually equilibrate with all of the body's sodium space. Similarly, radioactive potassium will eventually equilibrate in the body's potassium space. By taking blood samples after equilibration, we could estimate the total amount of exchangeable sodium or potassium in the body. Growing out of our studies on blood-volume determinations, we administered labeled serum protein intravenously and within a few days it distributed throughout the extracellular space. Thus, we were able first to measure the space of distribution of plasma in the circulation; then the subsequent loss of labeled albumin from the plasma meant that it was equilibrating in a larger body pool called the extracellular space. From the curves of disappearance of radioactivity from plasma we were able to make determinations of the rate of degradation and, by inferring that we were in steady-state conditions, the rate of production of body albumin and similarly of other serum proteins.

Arthur Mirsky, who was a distinguished diabetologist, suggested in 1952 that the disease diabetes might be caused by abnormally rapid degradation of insulin.[10] This suggestion was a very reasonable one because it was already known that the pancreas of adult diabetic subjects contained almost normal, and even on occasion, above normal amounts of insulin. On the other hand, it was generally assumed that all diabetics had an absolute deficiency of circulating insulin. This was a perfectly reasonable assumption, since in the 1950s the vast majority of diabetic subjects whose symptoms could not be controlled by diet alone received insulin.

If the pancreas has enough insulin and you assume the circulation has too little, then clearly the suggestion of abnormal degradation of insulin was a very reasonable one. We, therefore, thought that we could use the same techniques that we had used previously to study the turnover of labeled albumin to study the turnover of labeled insulin to see if the defect was in the insulin degradation rate. If insulin were abnormally degraded in the diabetic subject, then the labeled insulin should disappear from the plasma more rapidly than from the plasma of a nondiabetic subject.

To our surprise, the rate of disappearance of labeled insulin from the plasma of the vast majority of diabetic subjects was much slower, not faster, than from the vast majority of nondiabetic subjects. If we examined both groups more closely, we noted that in the slow-disappearing group there were schizophrenic subjects who had had a previous history of insulin shock therapy for the treatment of schizophrenia. Included in the rapidly disappearing group, there were some diabetic subjects who either did not require insulin therapy or who came to our laboratory very soon after diabetes had been discovered and before therapy had been instituted. Note the patient MN in figure 37. When he first came to our laboratory, the injected radioinsulin was rapidly disappearing and four months later in a similar study it was slowly disappearing.

Another group of diabetologists made the same observation at the same time we did. As the luck of science has it, they decided there was something in diabetes that resulted in retarding the rate of insulin disappearance. Because we made these other observations, such as the schizophrenic subject with insulin shock therapy, we recognized that the difference between the two groups was not a history of diabetes per se, but rather a history of previous insulin therapy. The fact that most diabetics received insulin therapy, and practically no nondiabetics did, was the important difference. We therefore made what we thought was a very reasonable assumption that the insulin in the treated subjects was bound to an antibody, which developed in response to treatment with a foreign protein.

After injection, insulin, 6,000 in molecular weight, was bound to antibodies, i.e., gamma-globulin, 160,000 in molecular weight. This big protein complex was not likely to leave the circulation very rapidly, whereas 6,000-molecular-weight insulin could escape. This fact could account for the slow disappearance of the insulin from the plasma of the insulin-treated subject. These experiments were made in the mid-1950s. Insulin was discovered and its use in treatment was begun in 1921. How could the observation of the antigenicity of insulin be missed for thirty-five years, when

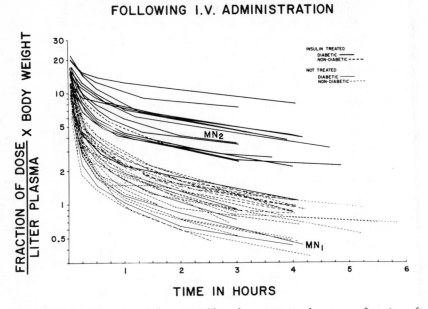

Figure 37. Trichloroactic acid precipitable radioactivity in plasma as a function of time following intravenous administration of ¹³¹I-insulin-treated and non-insulin-treated subjects. The disappearance was retarded in the insulin-treated subjects irrespective of whether they had received the hormone for treatment of diabetes or for shock therapy for schizophrenia. The retarded rate is a consequence of binding to insulin antibodies generated in response to administration of animal insulins. Note the slower disappearance from the plasma of MN after four months of insulin (curve MN_2) than prior to such therapy (curve MN_1). [© 1978 by The Nobel Foundation]

insulin therapy had been used in millions of subjects? Clearly, the concentration of insulin-binding antibodies must be so low that it would be missed by the classical techniques. Therefore, we undertook to develop new techniques employing the sensitivity of radioisotopic methods in order to determine whether or not there was insulin antibody in the circulation.

The first of the techniques that we used was paper electrophoresis. Free-labeled insulin, as is common with many peptides, with lysine and arginine residues, binds to paper at the site of application. We noted in the plasma of an insulin-treated subject that radioactivity migrated in whole or part as an inter beta-gamma-globulin. On starch block electrophoresis, in which starch simply provides the support, the labeled insulin migrated with virtually its free electrophoretic mobility, close to the albumin region. It's also retarded in the inter beta-gamma-globulin region in the plasma of immune subjects.

It was an interesting observation. We felt it necessary to test hundreds and thousands of plasmas from insulin-treated and nontreated subjects. These techniques were a big nuisance since they took overnight and were hard to deal with. I hate to say it, but we started this before automatic paper-strip counters were available. In order to make our observations, we would sit and cut up these paper strips into twelve parts to find out where the labeled insulin was. There had to be a better way; so we developed a very simple technique with a fancy name, chromatoelectrophoresis. We left the top of the electrophoresis box open, increased the voltage to heat the paper strips. The water evaporated from the paper strips, drawing the serum proteins in towards the center. The labeled insulin that was bound to the paper remained at the site of application, but all the other serum proteins migrated *in toto* with essentially water-flow chromatography. By combining chromatography with electrophoresis, we could effect separation in the cold room in about half an hour instead of overnight. Not only that, but we could cut into two places rather than in twelve places to determine where the labeled insulin was, as had been necessary for standard paper electrophoresis. Thus, with so simple a modification of methodology, we were able to examine hundreds and thousands of such samples. In our laboratory, we have never found a patient without a previous history of insulin therapy who had what we called the insulin-binding globulin.

Return to the patient MN-1, the rapid disappearer who converted into a slow disappearer. We were able to demonstrate that initially in his plasma the labeled insulin bound to paper at the site of application. We were able to demonstrate subsequently with a new type of strip counter that the labeled insulin in plasma taken after months of insulin therapy migrated in part in the inter beta-gamma region. We then used a variety of physical-chemical systems to test further the binding of insulin to globulins. We used ultracentrifugation, the antibody-bound insulin sedimented very rapidly in the ultracentrifuge, because it was high in molecular weight. The free insulin did not sediment rapidly. We used salt fractionation techniques to separate bound and free insulins. We used at least half a dozen other physical-chemical systems. We were able to demonstrate with these different methods the development of an insulin-binding globulin, which we thought was antibody, in the plasma-treated subjects.

In 1955 we submitted the paper to *Science*, just as Duane Roller was leaving the editorship. The paper was held there for eight months before it was reviewed. It was finally rejected. We submitted it to the *Journal of Clinical Investigation*, which also rejected it. But I had the faith typical of a scientist and I saved the letter of rejection, which said that "this was already the second revision." We had used the words "insulin-transporting antibody in the circulation of insulin-treated subjects." The reviewers rejected our conclusion that it was an antibody. They rejected it largely on the basis that if you read the classic textbooks of immunology, the phrase was repeated frequently, that peptides smaller than 10,000 molecular weight could not be antigenic. Insulin was 6,000 in molecular weight and, therefore, could not be antigenic.

Finally, the paper was accepted with revisions. Calling it "insulin-binding globulin" was a compromise.[11] We were permitted to insert a small paragraph—anyone who reads the 1956 *Journal of Clinical Investigation* may wonder why Sol Berson and I put in that paragraph—in which we quoted from a standard textbook of *Immunology and Bacteriology* the definition of an antibody and cited the proof of how we met each of these criteria.

This discovery of antibody to a small peptide really effected a revolution in immunology. We now appreciate that peptides as small as the octapeptides, vasopressin, and oxytocin are antigenic in some species. The use of radio-isotopic methods permits us to determine the equilibrium constant of the reaction of antigen with antibody at the level of 10^{-14} liters mole^{-1}, whereas classic, immunological methods do not permit determinations of less than 10^{-6}.

In this famous rejected paper also, there was a description of what later became the radioimmunoassay principle. In order to determine the concentration of antibody in the circulation, we used what one might call saturation analysis. We increased the concentration of insulin, using the labeled insulin as a tracer to find how much insulin could be bound to antibody [fig. 38]. As we increased the concentration of insulin from 0.75 milliunits per milliliter up to a number ten-fold higher, we reduced the ratio of antibody bound to free radioactive insulin from 2 to 1 to 1 to 2. This provided the basis of the radioimmunoassay principle.

However, we knew that the concentration that we were able to measure, on the order of a milliunit of insulin per milliliter, did not provide the sensitivity that was needed to measure plasma insulin in man. It was known that pancreatectomized subjects have insulin requirements on the order of thirty to fifty units of insulin per day. From our studies of the distribution and turnover of labeled insulin, we knew the rate at which insulin was metabolized. Therefore, we calculated that the peak insulin concentration should be of the order of 100 microunits per milliliter; we were off by a factor of ten fold.

In the days in which research was less competitive, it was actually three years before we were able to demonstrate that the use of guinea pig antisera, rather than human antisera, provided the sensitivity needed. We now know that guinea pig antisera were most suitable because guinea pig insulin differs from human insulin in multiple sites, multiple amino acids, whereas rabbit and human insulin differ from pork insulin only in a single amino acid at the terminal end of the B-chain.

For the uninitiated, the radioimmunoassay principle operates this way [fig. 39]: let's consider only two antibody molecules and let's assume that we have eight labeled insulin molecules. Assuming equilibrium, at most we can put four of the labeled insulin molecules on these four antibody binding sites.

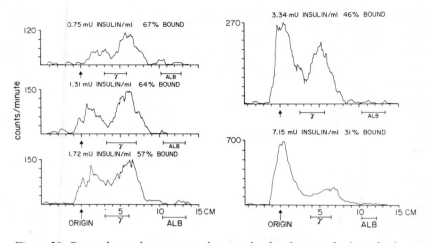

Figure 38. Paper electrophoretograms showing the distribution of ^{131}I-insulin between that bound to antibody (migrating with serum protection) and that free (remaining at site of application) in the presence of increasing concentration of labeled insulin. The antibodies were from an insulin-treated human subject. [© 1978 by The Nobel Foundation]

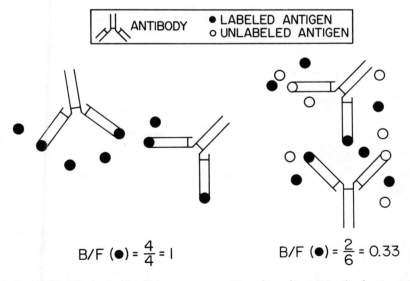

Figure 39. The basis of radioimmunoassay. Note the reduction in the fraction of the radiolabeled antigen bound to antibody in the presence of an increased amount of unlabeled antigen.

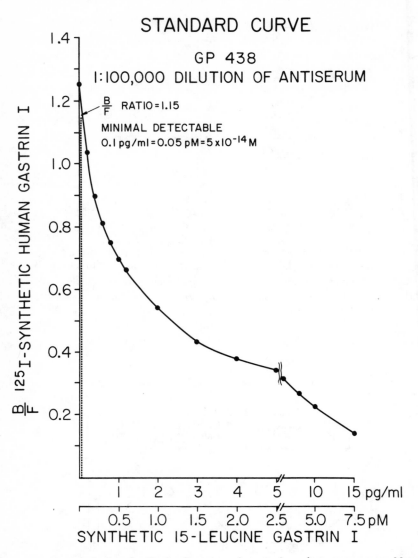

Figure 40. Standard curve for the detection of gastrin by radioimmunoassay. Note that as little as 0.2 pg gastrin/ml incubation mixture (0.1 picomolar) is readily detectable. [© 1978 by The Nobel Foundation]

The antibody bound to free ratio is one. If we now double the amount of insulin by adding an equivalent amount of unlabeled insulin to the labeled insulin, only two of the radioactive molecules can find their way onto the antibody-binding site. We reduce the ratio of bound to free to 0.33. With very large excess of unlabeled insulin, virtually none of the radioactive insulin can be bound. This is a simple way of looking at it.

To perform a radioimmunoassay, one prepares a standard curve [fig. 40] with a series of tubes containing a fixed amount of labeled antigen and antibody. Known amounts of antigen, i.e., the stable insulin being measured, are added in increasing amounts. The ratio of antibody bound to free radioinsulin decreases in the presence of increasing amounts of insulin. From the standard curve we can determine the concentration in the unknown samples. This is the radioimmunoassay principle. It's very simple, we just determine the behavior of the unknown samples compared to that of known standards in inhibiting the binding of labeled antigen to antibody.

We first applied radioimmunoassay to measuring the insulin response in early-maturity-onset diabetics. We gave patients a glucose load. Diabetes is characterized by a slight delay in insulin response. However, we found the Mirsky hypothesis was wrong.[12] The fact is that the diabetic subject with an adequate amount of insulin in his pancreas released an excessive amount of insulin in response to continued hyperglycemia. We now know that many maturity-onset diabetics are characterized not by an absolute insulin deficiency, but by the failure of their bodies to respond appropriately to their insulin. Something is wrong with their insulin sensitivity and not in the insulin levels.

Radioimmunoassay is now used to measure hundreds of substances of biologic interest, including the following:

PEPTIDAL HORMONES

Pituitary Hormones
Growth hormone
Adrenocorticotropic hormone (ACTH)
Melanocyte stimulating hormone (MSH)
  α-MSH
  β-MSH
Glycoproteins
  Thyroid stimulating hormone (TSH)
  Follicle stimulating hormone (FSH)
  Luteinizing hormone (LH)
Prolactin
Lipotropin
Vasopressin
Oxytocin
Chorionic Hormones
Human chorionic gonadotropin (HCG)
Human chorionic somatomammotropin (HCS)
Pancreatic Hormones
Insulin

Glucagon
Pancreatic Polypeptide
Calcitropic Hormones
Parathyroid hormone (PTH)
Calcitonin (CT)
Gastrointestinal Hormones
Gastrin
Secretin
Cholecystokinin (CCK)
Vasoactive intestinal polypeptide (VIP)
Gastric inhibitory polypeptide (GIP)
Vasoactive Tissue Hormones
Angiotensins
Bradykinins
Releasing and Release Inhibiting Factors
Thyrotropin releasing factor (TRF)
LHRF
Somatostatin
Other Peptides
Substance P
Endorphins
Enkephalins

NON-PEPTIDAL HORMONES

Thyroidal Hormones
Thyroxine (T_4)
Triiodothyronine (T_3)
Reverse T_3
Steroids
Aldosterone
Corticosteroids
Estrogens
Androgens
Progesterones
Prostaglandins
Biologic Amines
Serotonin
Melatonin

NON-HORMONAL SUBSTANCES

Drugs & Vitamins
Cardiac glycosides
Drugs of Abuse
Psychoactive Drugs
Antibiotics
CNS Depressants
Vitamin A, Folic acid
Cyclic Nucleotides
Enzymes
C_1 esterase
Fructose 1, 6 diphosphatase

Plasminogen, Plasmin
Chymotrypsin, Trypsin
Carbonic anhydrase isoenzymes
Aldose reductase
Carboxypeptidase B
Pancreatic elastase
Viruses
Hepatitis associated antigen
Murine Leukemia viruses
    (Gross, Rauscher, Moloney)
Mason-Pfizer monkey virus
Tumor Antigens
Carcinoembryonic antigen
α-Fetoprotein
Serum Proteins
Thyroxine binding globulin
IgG, IgE, IgA, IgM
Properdin
Fibrinogen
Apolipoprotein B
Myoglobin
Myelin Basic Protein
Other
Intrinsic factor
Rheumatoid factor
Hageman factor
Neurophysins
Staphylococcal
    β-Enterotoxin

Radioimmunoassay first gave us new insights into endocrinology. The concentrations of peptide hormones in the non-stimulated state range from a low of 10^{-12} molar to a high of 10^{-10} molar. Chemically, the peptide hormones look like the proteins present in billion-fold higher concentration, so chemical methods cannot be used for their measurement. Bioassays for some of them did exist, for ACTH and for insulin. With radioimmunoassay we can measure in a drop of blood what used to take a liter of blood. The method was required for such substances as the peptide hormones.

It's also used for the nonpeptidal hormones. Classical chemical methods some thirty years ago could measure thyroxine in the circulation, but these were difficult. Hypothyroidism is associated with a decrease in circulating thyroxine. In the United States, one in four thousand children suffers from neonatal hypothyroidism, underactivity of the thyroid of the new born. If these children aren't treated within a month or so, they are irreversibly mentally retarded. A heel prick, a drop of blood on a piece of filter paper, and with radioimmunoassay we can make this diagnosis within a week after birth. The cost of this radioimmunoassay in government laboratories runs to about one dollar a sample. The disease is easy to treat at a cost of about one dollar a year. For $5,000 each year, we can identify and improve the mental capacity of these children for whom diagnosis could not have been made without radioimmunoassay. From a public health point of view, this has been the most important benefit from our work. With radioimmunoassay, virtually any organic substance of biological interest can eventually be measured.

It's been a long way for a girl born of immigrant parents, who aspired for her to be an elementary school teacher, because that's what was done in New York at that time. My father graduated from eighth grade and went to work. When my mother came from Germany, she went to a small town in Wellsville, Ohio, and when she graduated from sixth grade she came to New York and went to work. They knew their children would go through college, but they didn't know what physics was. Coming through the New York City public school system, going to a New York City public college, inspired by my teachers, trained by the literature that was available to me, I knew there was a way up and I found it. I've been very happy with it.

I'm a scientist because even at this stage I love investigation. Even after the Nobel Prize, the biggest thrill is to go to my laboratory and hope that that day I will know something nobody ever knew before. There are very few days when it happens, but the dream is still there. That's what it means to be an investigator.

Geophysics

J. TUZO WILSON

Director-General, Ontario Science Centre; fellow, Massey College, University of Toronto; foreign associate, National Academy of Sciences (U.S.); recipient of Bucher Medal, American Geophysical Union, Logan Medal, Geological Association of Canada, Penrose Medal, Geological Society of America, Carty Medal, National Academy of Sciences.

"I entered college to take physics and chemistry but . . . the geology that Noel Odell, then fresh from Mount Everest, showed me in the summer so fascinated me that when I returned for my second year, I told my shocked professors that I thought . . . their subjects were circumscribed and tedious and that I wanted to switch to geology. . . . I was grudgingly allowed to be the first student to take both physics and geology leading to geophysics. . . . I now realize that if anything can be done differently, in a way that is more energetic and involves change and excitement, that is the way I seem bound to pursue. . . .

"To recognize regularities one should look at the earth as a whole on an earth-sized scale and not on a man-sized scale; [that] led me to try to synthesize, to plot the glacial and tectonic features of Canada, using air photographs when they first became available, to study the Precambrian Shields and great faults of the world, to compare oceanic islands and the linear chains and island arcs they form, and finally to get a glimmer of the great plates of the earth's crust. In the process I was able to travel widely and became embroiled in international exchanges. . . ."

My life has been a joyful one and research has added to its jubilations. On the face of it, my life has been normal, almost prosaic. I had a quiet upbringing. I went to a university. I didn't do anything very special there. I was in the Geological Survey of Canada and in the Canadian Army for a few years each and then I spent a long time as a professor. Eventually I went on to administrative jobs.

It would appear to have been a quiet life, and research to have been added as a sort of icing. In reality, my life has been exceedingly exciting. I had the luck to be active when new ideas were breaking, and to have had appropriate training to grasp the opportunities.

Before describing any of these excitements I shall describe how I entered research, and mention some influences that affected my work. In science, it is necessary to think in appropriate scales. This only dawned on me gradually. As humans, we think of things on our own scale. However, we know that one's senses can delude one. Magicians and many actors make a living out of giving people false impressions. Science produces the same effects. If one turns to the very small, the rules of common sense, Euclidean geometry, and time do not apply. Einstein also showed brilliantly how these rules are changed when one considers the universe as a whole.

Darwin realized that man had not been created by a sudden act of God in God's image, which had long been the common-sense view, but had evolved over very long periods of time from other creatures. This was a heretical statement, contrary to conventional wisdom. Going farther back, Copernicus had made the initial step that made modern science possible when he concluded that the earth was not situated on a pillar in the middle of the universe with all the heavens going around it on crystal spheres. As long as people believed that—they believed it very sincerely 500 years ago— they couldn't really get very far with mechanics, gravity, or the fundamentals of science. This is not to say that no science was successful before. I would remind you that Ptolemaic astronomers had been navigators for Magellan and Columbus; they predicted eclipses and they invented the calendar we use today. These things were not destroyed by the Copernican revolution, which changed the way men look at the solar system and the universe.

In geology it's not necessary to change geometry or to depart from the laws of classical physics. It's simply hard to conceive of the very long time scale. Also, the earth is one of those objects that cannot be brought into the laboratory. Most of the things studied in physics, chemistry, and biology can be studied in the laboratory. This is not so of the earth. Geology used to be done on a man-sized scale. One went out and mapped an area, collected and studied some fossils and minerals, but the earth is a bigger thing than that. One needs to look at the earth on the earth-sized scale. One needs to look at the universe on the universe-sized scale. One can't go out and examine it, so Einstein's achievement was a tremendous one. In geology, it is possible to go out and look at the world. This necessity for leaving the laboratory obviously makes a big difference in the type of life one leads and one's viewpoint differs from that of laboratory scientists or astronomers.

The slow dawning of this idea has been a major influence in my life, one that has affected my research and assisted in changing my ideas. I shall now describe my entry into science. Though I'm a Canadian and many of my ancestors have been Canadians or Americans for many generations, in the summer of 1913 my mother took me to Europe to visit relatives. Although a small boy, I remember this clearly. I stayed in rural England, the country which then ruled a quarter of the earth's surface and was the greatest power on earth. I recall the leisurely Edwardian country life, such as Galsworthy had described. Gentlemen wore silk hats and ladies' dresses swept the ground. Since 1913 there have been enormous changes in health, transportation, communication, food, leisure, and manners, but I don't know that this has changed enjoyment.

Having been brought up largely during World War I, I had to work very hard. I walked four miles every day, going back and forth to school. There were no school busses. In the summers as a high school student, and as a freshman taking physics and chemistry, I was fortunate to go out in the field. I came to love that life and there, a geologist, Noel Odell, showed me the beauties of geology. The autumn after my freshman year, I went back to university and said I thought that physics and chemistry were not very exciting compared to geology. This upset the Department of Physics very much indeed. Physics was then in its heyday. It was never imagined that anyone capable of doing physics would prefer geology.

Geology was in a dismal state. Continental drift had not been accepted, and the study of geology consisted of making maps and collecting minerals and fossils. No theory was allowed. Theory was scornfully termed armchair geology and was always unsuccessful. The earth was considered to be a static body, and therefore one couldn't theorize successfully because it actually *is* a mobile body. This idea had been put forward by the German geophysicist Alfred Wegener in the year I was born, and by Frank Taylor, an American, but I was too stupid to accept this idea until I was fifty.

Nevertheless, from the point of view of a physicist, I could see that something was wrong with geology. Lord Rutherford[1] said it was like postage stamp collecting. Physics depended on the glory of its laws, which were precise, enabled one to make predictions, and could be verified, while geology had no use at all for theory. I respected physics, but I loved geology. Even though I recognized it was somewhat like making love to a beautiful but half-witted girl. As long as nobody spoke, everything was fine.

There were intellectual advantages to looking at geology from the point of view of a physicist, and looking at physics from the point of view of geologist, but personal disadvantages, because geologists were sensitive to the fact that they had had a lack of success in their science, while the physicists did not like their subject being regarded as a tool and I always looked at physics to see how one could use any development to study the earth.

Another advantage I should mention for the benefit of any high school students here: I had the good fortune to be the first person to graduate in a course in geophysics in Canada. Today in Canada, and of course in the United States, hundreds of people graduate in geophysics. There were some geophysicists before that time, but they had come in as adults and taught themselves the subject. The idea of having courses in geophysics was new; it was a great advantage to be early.

Turning now to some of the excitement. I went at the age of fifteen to the woods, to the north country. Over the years in studying geology I've spent a thousand nights under canvas and under the stars. Incidentally, I learned canoeing, portaging, skiing, and climbing. This was very exciting. It opened my eyes to the fact that life in cities is not the only life. It may sound strange, but three summers running, I've had my hands on a live moose in the woods. The moose, of course, were swimming and I was paddling. One can paddle faster than a moose swims, and it's exciting to take hold of a moose. It's even more exciting to jump out of a canoe on to their backs. And when wild ducks are moulting, they can't take off, so by running after them in swamps one can catch them. In 1934 I climbed a 12,000-foot mountain in Montana, which the people in the neighborhood didn't think had been climbed, and there was very good local evidence to show that nobody had ever been on the summit there before.

I've been guided by birch bark notes to find the survivor of two men, one of whom had been drowned 100 miles from anywhere in the Northwest Territories. I've built igloos and slept in them, sharing with Eskimo families a supper of dried fish and seal meat that they had caught and cooked over a stone lamp with the fat of those same seals. We slept comfortably on caribou skins. The parents of those Eskimos had lived in the days when some people starved to death because they didn't catch enough to eat. All these experiences give one a different perspective on life from what one encounters today in the cities.

Immediately after World War II, four-engine planes were available for the first time and I was on three long flights over the Arctic Sea looking for unknown islands. None were found on those flights, but on others some of my companions did find the last islands to be added to the map of North America.

Another thing that influenced me was that on returning from World War II a wise man said to me, "Don't accept any administrative positions. Go back to the university and do research for twenty years." I followed that advice. In 1948 he also arranged for me to go to my first international scientific meeting. This led to greatly increased opportunities for travel. Last year, for example, I did 70,000 miles and I've been doing that amount of traveling for many years. This has enabled me to see the earth pretty well, from the North Pole to Antarctica.

In 1950 in New Guinea, the district officers who looked after me were still establishing contact with tribes that had never before had any contact with the outside world. In 1958 I rode the Trans-Siberian Railway from Moscow to Peking to become a guest of the People's Republic of China. I've been benighted several times, once in an African rift valley in a grass hut with hyenas howling outside. I became a pilot and learned to use early aerial photographs. This was all very exciting and I'm sure it doesn't sound much like research. For physicists, chemists, and many biologists it would have been a pleasant waste of time, but for a geologist it was valuable to see so much of the world. The combination of having a background in physics, which had provided me with a quantitative point of view, and of having traveled a great deal, has been important in helping me to change attitudes. The revolution in the earth sciences, which the acceptance of continental drift represented, was largely achieved by a group of people who had in common the fact that they traveled widely and had a more quantitative training than other geologists.

I came to believe that the old way of studying geology, although the geologists said they were studying the physiology of the earth, was wrong. In practice, all they were doing, if the earth had been a rabbit, would have been counting the hairs on its back. They weren't studying its physiology; they were looking at superficial details.

Those who contributed most to changing attitudes included physicists like Wegener and Ewing and Vine;[2] geologists like du Toit, who was also a surveyor; Arthur Holmes, who was also a chemist and who made some of the first radiometric age determinations; and Harry Hess, whose mind was sufficiently quantitative that he was at one time head of the Advisory Committee on the Space Program. These men all had a combination of geology and physics in their background, and they had all traveled a great deal.

Because of similar influences, I too tried to look at the earth as a whole. My research took the form of synthesis. I was a member of the committee that produced the first tectonic map and the first glacial map of all Canada. Both are very different from those in the United States, the latter because ice sheets act like conveyor belts. Canada is where the ice sheets formed and picked up debris and the United States is where they melted and dumped it. The results are quite different, which at first surprised us. We did most of this research by using aerial photographs. We discovered that one didn't have to examine everything in the field. Once one had found out what glacial features looked like in aerial photographs, one could look at the photographs and plot features very much more quickly than by plodding around the North Country and mapping. At the time this was considered heresy and unsound.

Structures began to interest me. Not only the faults, folds, and age of the Canadian shield, but those of all the shields. The nature of island arcs also intrigued me. Why are there so many circular arcs on the surface of the sphere? Why are there other linear chains of ocean islands? What had formed the great faults of the world? I tried to study them on a large scale, which I thought to be the appropriate scale upon which to understand the earth. As a consequence of these studies I was forced to become a convert to Wegener's views. In middle age this was an agonizing experience. At the three universities I had attended these ideas had been dismissed as absolute, addlepated nonsense. Wegener was disregarded. It was not that anyone had ever proven him wrong. His was such heresy that you didn't speak or think seriously about it. To change and accept Wegener's views involved a difficult reversal in philosophical attitude, but when eventually each of us came to accept the new theory, each one could suddenly make a great step forward. As a result, I would agree with Dr. Yalow that the greatest joy research can provide is to enable one occasionally to think that for a short time one might have had an original idea. In comparison with the satisfaction of having had a good idea it does not much matter after that whether it gets published, accepted, or whether anyone else agrees. Such an achievement gives confidence to speak out in favor of what one believes to be true, even if it's contrary to current dogma. Another satisfaction that comes out of completion of one piece of successful research is that it provides the opportunity to move on to other fields. I had already moved about a good deal in geology, from Precambrian geology to glacial and then to plate tectonics, but greater changes were possible. After twenty years in research at the university, the president asked me if I would care to start a new campus of the University of Toronto. I said, "No, I like being a professor, I don't want to do that." He said, "The campus we're starting at Erindale covers about 300 very pleasant acres. Have you been there? Have you ever seen it?" I said, "No." He said, "Why don't you take your wife, Isabel, to look at it, see what she says, and give me your decision after the weekend?" I said, "That seems reasonable."

Erindale was indeed a lovely place, and it included a beautiful estate and house, 100 years old, where we were expected to live. In May the trees and gardens were at their best. Isabel took one look and said, "Jock, this is just the job for you." I thought she might be right, for possibly such an occasion wouldn't occur again. I'd been an academic for a long time, had my minor successes in research, and it was my turn to do a little administration. It also seemed appropriate, if one believes that a university should be run by academics and not by businessmen. I accepted.

Fortunately, it was a subsidiary campus so I didn't have any direct dealings with the board of governors or any fund raising. I dealt with the president, his minions, and with the architect. There were a lot of interesting aspects to this which were not scientific research, but which in many ways seemed to be related kinds of investigation, so that experience and training in scientific research, and some confidence gained from it, helped me. For example, the architect produced a first set of plans that to me seemed confused. I took them to a psychiatrist and, with his help, we persuaded the architect and the university authorities to scrap the $118,000 worth of plans and start all over again on a simpler plan. As a result, we had a much more human design for the buildings, instead of a monument to the architect. It was something that people could live in.

Later it also occurred to me, after I had read Kuhn's book *Structure of Scientific Revolutions*,[3] and concluded that I had been involved in one—the acceptance of plate tectonics and continental drift—what a fortunate thing it is for a scientist to be involved in a science that's undergoing a revolution, because it's much easier to make a reputation when everything's changing than it is in the normal course of events.

I looked around, but I didn't see any fresh fields in science in which to try to make a reputation. Maybe there were some, but I couldn't see any. Isaac Asimov thinks the study of the brain is due for a revolution, but I think that economics is the field that needs one. It seems to fit the requirements perfectly. Just as geology, when I was a young man, had been full of contradictory and inaccurate prediction, so is economics today. It is very sad that the leaders of government, business, and industry are so imbued with ideas of growth that they make all sorts of statements about how desirable it would be to have 5 percent annual growth forever. They even seem to think that we can curtail scientific research and still have 5 percent growth. They don't seem to know what they're talking about because in the latter years their predictions have not been correct.

The basic reason is that they've forgotten the causes of the prosperity of the last 200 years. I'm very much aware of the advantages of the growth that has taken place. I've lived through one-third of it, more than the last sixty-six years. I can see the changes since 1913, and it's been a good thing indeed. I can quite see why people would hope it would continue. But this doesn't necessarily mean that it *will* continue. The mistake is they don't realize that it was not the idea of Adam Smith nor the idea of the Declaration of Independence 200 years ago that caused economic growth. Many people say that, but I think it to be nonsense. It was James Watt who was the real creator of the Wealth of Nations. It was the invention and discovery of synthetic power, the steam engine and subsequently other forms of synthetic power, that made possible our present prosperity. It was not dependence upon the notions of industrial capitalism or of democracy. These more or less followed, because wealth had made them possible.

It is hard to imagine now, but 200 years ago, slavery was common. This was because muscle power, wind power and waterpower were the only kinds of power that there were. The use of our modern science, and the source of our modern affluence, have come from the fact that we have plenty of power to build things with and to turn our resources to use. Technologists and scientists were the originators of our present affluence. This fact is lost sight of because scientists and engineers are quite happy to remain in their laboratories. Their joys are quite different from those of other people. Once a discovery, like a steam engine or a motor car or an internal combustion engine, has been made, other people take over. They are lawyers, business-men, and government officials, and they take over and run things. They are the people who really dictate what goes on, and they take a short-term view.

This is unfortunate. There are too few scientists in government and the results are not always what we might wish.

I'm sure that growth cannot long continue. This can be understood very easily by a simple analogy. Businessmen say that the desirable rate of growth is 5 percent and that we must have it. Imagine that the human being could grow at the rate of 5 percent a year, steadily throughout its lifetime. A newly born infant is eighteen or twenty inches long. Five percent of twenty inches is one inch, so in its first year it grows an inch. Anybody who has anything to do with children realizes that's not very good. One inch a year is not adequate, so 5 percent is much too small for a human being. That's too slow a growth. However, if the child continues to survive and grow, it will grow a little each year. This will add up, so by the age of fifteen, it will be about three feet high. It will still be a dwarf. Not only would the parents be distressed but the child will be also.

However, now it's growing two inches a year and it will double in another fifteen years. By the age of thirty, it will be six feet tall and growing four inches a year. That's just great. The average rate, which had been too slow at the beginning, has turned out to be just right. Over a period of thirty years, it turns out that 5 percent has been just right. Remember, however, we said the child keeps on growing and as an adult grows 5 percent also. It would double again at age forty-five, sixty, seventy-five, and if the person lived that long, at ninety years. At these ages, it would become twelve, twenty-four, forty-eight, and ninety-six feet tall. Fortunately, we stopped growing. We're rather happy about it and we don't think we stopped living at twenty when we stopped growing and became no-growth humans. No one is unhappy and we're still alive and enjoying life without growth.

Now, because 5 percent was good in our youth and because in the early history of North America 5 percent was too slow when the first man stepped off Columbus's ship, it doesn't mean that we can continue to grow at the 5 percent rate in perpetuity, and yet the economists, the leaders in government, business, and industry, if you read the financial pages, argue this every day. They don't seem to realize—and it astonishes me—that accountants and bankers, who should know about figures, do not calculate the results. They are as blind as we geologists were. It's a heresy to question 5 percent growth. Five percent is holy, so one doesn't think about it. Everyone accepts 5 percent as proper and accepts that it's going to keep on.

Actually, no growth is not exceptional. We're not advocating the end of things. It's normal. Nature lives in a state of no growth. If you imagine a primitive forest in a jungle and return there century after century, it continues to look the same. All the animals, trees, and plants in that area are going to be replaced. The overall size remains the same. People think that a no-growth economy would be stagnant. A jungle isn't a stagnant place. Another good example of a no-growth economy in miniature is a poker game. At the end of a poker game, there are the same number of players very often, the same number of cards, the same number of chips, and the same amount of money as there was in the beginning. Some people have lost and some people have won. Everybody has had quite an exciting time. A no-growth economy, far from being stagnant, might be even more exciting than the ones we're used to!

The reason economics is not a science is not because you can't apply mathematics to it. It's because the economist won't accept the conclusions! It's exactly the same trouble that affected us in geology. We wouldn't accept the idea of continental drift. It's the same thing that happened before Copernicus, before Darwin, before Einstein. A scientific revolution is needed.

Another field that is right for a scientific revolution is the social sciences. What form does this take? One probably has to accept nature's laws instead of the ethical ones we prefer. I'm not prepared to recommend that, so I'm not recommending that we have a scientific revolution of the social sciences, but I do recommend that we have one in economics—as Malthus long ago realized.

Since leaving Erindale six years ago I have been in charge of a science center. It is not a museum of the past but a place devoted to modern science. It educates people, both children who come in free classes and adults who pay to come, about what's going on in the world today. This is a very fascinating and useful pursuit because science is generally neglected in schools. It is generally not well taught at the elementary level because most people in elementary schools have not had much training in science themselves. They have to pass on something they don't understand very well.

Take, for example, our ability to predict the future. Many have an idea that the future automatically is going to be the same as the past. This presents a very great danger for all nations. To predict things solely from the past is a dangerous activity. It's dangerous to the whole Western world. I think that possibly some of these scientific ideas, which are not research themselves but arise from having spent some time in research, are useful concepts to present in a science center. It's very important that there be centers devoted to teaching people about the facts of modern science as well as about the glories of the past. We need to present the joys of research, since discovering new ideas is the most exciting thing one can do. In addition, we need to convey that the ideas of research should be applied to broader fields. This application may not be one of the joys of research because some of the conclusions may be gloomy.

Consider the concerns that are arising from ideas developing about the limits of growth. Just as the early colonists did not see any limit because they didn't know very well where the Pacific Ocean was and thought that the United States went on forever, nevertheless there was a limit. In research we are beginning to see that there are limits, not necessarily everywhere, but there are some limits to the unending frontiers in research. By this I mean, for one thing, that not everybody who wants to do research is going to be able to do it, because the growth of research has been faster than the economy.

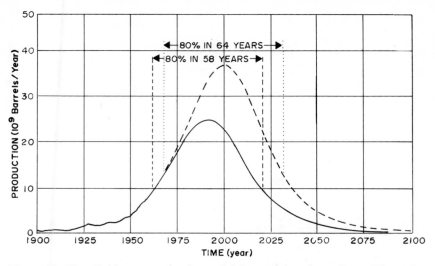

Figure 41. King Hubbert curve for the availability and use of petroleum. The cycle of world oil production is plotted on the basis of two estimates of the amount of oil that will ultimately be produced. The upper curve reflects Ryman's estimate of $2,100 \times 10^9$ barrels and the lower curve represents an estimate of $1,350 \times 10^9$ barrels.

If the economy is going to drop off or level off, there will be corresponding changes in research support. Like energy reserves, a declining curve is not the only possible curve, but neither can continue to grow forever. It is possible that either could reach a peak, and by discovery of fresh sources of energy could remain at a high level. We are near the peak for petroleum, perhaps, but there are other sources besides petroleum in this world. Such a curve was drawn by King Hubbert for petroleum [fig. 41].[4]

However, it seems to me that we cannot expect to keep on expanding, and even though more and more people are being trained in research, there may not be more jobs in research. The competition is going to make life more difficult for students. It doesn't mean there will be no research. It may even mean a slow increase in research. Nevertheless, it does mean that not everybody who wants to get into research is necessarily going to. It may be harder to get a position. There will be opportunities to find new fields of research. There's lots of scope in fields such as economics, and this is certainly a very good place for young people to go.

It's always hard to break into traditional fields, but it may be possible to find new fields in which to apply scientific methods. One of these fields may be in pedagogy. It is sad that so much of the teaching about science, which is so very exciting to all of us scientists, should in school appear to be dull and difficult. Science is not dull and difficult. Some scientists are dull and difficult, and certainly many people who teach science are dull and difficult. There must be scope for improving pedagogy in the schools in science. Above all, science has changed so rapidly that there's a very fascinating need to teach it so the public may better understand the problems this world faces. I'm optimistic that students will continue to discover new opportunities.

Yalow-Wilson Discussion

JAMES D. EBERT, Moderator

President, Carnegie Institution of Washington; board of directors, International Society of Developmental Biologists; member, National Academy of Sciences; consultant to the Aging Program, National Institute of Child Health and Human Development; judging committee, AAAS-Westinghouse Science Writing Awards. Former professor of biology and embryology, Johns Hopkins University, and director, Marine Biological Laboratory. Research in experimental embryology, developmental biology, cell biology, immunology, the biology of aging.

George Field: I found Professor Wilson's comments very stimulating, but I do think that he may have made a leap that is not justified. Consider economic growth measured in terms of, let us say, oil production, or of gross production of some quantity of goods. Indeed, he may be correct. That kind of growth may not continue for the reasons that he indicated. Nevertheless, it seems to me that there is another kind of growth, namely, the growth in ideas and the growth in new ways of solving problems. An example would be the increase in power of computation. At relatively little expenditure in gross energy or materials, one can fashion a device that can do enormously fast computations and data manipulation, which is revolutionizing all kinds of activities in human life. One can speculate about other revolutions of this kind born of science and technology. It seems to be an erroneous leap to make the assumption that because the gross production of goods measured in terms of barrels of oil is going to level off, human society will become a constant. I can envision a future in which human society continues to develop rapidly, as we have seen it do for 200 years, more or less into the indefinite future. Dr. Yalow's comments were especially pertinent, because she showed how by expenditure of brain effort, but not large quantities of energy or material, one can revolutionize the field of medicine. That would be an example of what I'm trying to say.

WILSON: I hope you are right. I realize there are examples of substitution of computation for things that require more labor and energy. I hope that this will take place, but it concerns me that the economists, bankers, and businessmen do not agree. Their insistence upon a 5 percent growth rate may deplete our resources too fast to allow this kind of development. What concerns me is not that the computations will not develop, and the skills will not develop, but what concerns me is that it may not be possible to adjust society. For example, will people living in our cities be able to continue to work since most people live in the suburbs and they soon may not have enough gas to continue to drive to work?

Participant: Dr. Yalow, concerning the difficulty of getting your and Dr. Berson's results in radioimmunoassay accepted, the reviewers said the work was suggestive but further research and justification were necessary. One thing I was always struck by was that in 1905 an insignificant patent clerk, outside the mainstream of academia, wrote three papers in a major journal of physics that revolutionized the way of thinking and were very different from other ways of thinking. They were accepted and published very quickly. He was unknown. What do you, Dr. Yalow, feel would happen today, if he posited such extraordinary and unusual results?

YALOW: I would say that much of the science of seventy years ago would not pass peer review systems today and not be funded. Einstein, of course, had the good fortune that he needed only his mind, pencil, and paper. Actually, the point you raised I was discussing with my husband this morning. How was a relative unknown able to get three papers published in the *Annalen der Physik* so easily? Perhaps it was because there weren't thousands of people filling it up with junk. [Laughter] It was easy to see what the real need was in scientific development.

Participant: It seems to me as a university history teacher that one of the problems with history has been exactly what Dr. Wilson spoke of—the King Hubbert curve on the board that we like very much to place on history. The model has a slow beginning, a rise of a civilization, it goes along at the top for awhile, and then it falls because that's a very easy thing to teach. But it would be extremely valuable were we to turn our attention to some systems that did not rise, come to a peak, and then fall. We ought to consider some closed systems, some systems that are in equilibrium. Perhaps that's a possible model of one way historians could go.

WILSON: I highly agree. I did make reference to the fact that it was possible to have such systems, but I didn't draw them. This is what King Hubbert knew from petroleum, but lots of other things don't follow. It would be possible to have a curve that reached a plateau, not in petroleum resources but in some other resources. But it seems to me that for twenty-five years now King Hubbert's predictions have been shown to be correct. We in Canada, Europe, and the United States perceive this. Yet, we're not taking adequate steps to arrive at such a better solution as you suggest is possible. I would agree it is possible.

Participant: An historical comment, on the question that was asked about Einstein's allegedly relative ease of publication. It should be remembered that although Einstein was working in a patent office, he had published several relatively respectable papers in the journals, and also, the editor of the *Annalen der Physik* was Max Planck.

Participant: Dr. Yalow, do you visualize that synthetic insulin, which is on the horizon, will still give rise to the antigenicity problem, the sensitivity that you spoke of?

YALOW: Synthetic insulin is possible with what we now know from recombinant DNA research. I have not been one who has supported the synthesis of insulin as a very significant contribution. If you consider that you can go to the drugstore and buy insulin at about 400 units for a dollar and if you bought the same volume of sterile saline, its cost would be the same, then the cost of insulin really is negligible. I think that biosynthetic procedures will not significantly reduce the cost of insulin. Our requirements for insulin also seem to increase with our requirements for meat. Therefore, it is very likely that the pancreas will continue to remain the primary source of insulin.

Recombinant DNA research should give us first the hormones that we would not otherwise have. The one that's most important is human growth hormone. We cannot use growth hormone from any animal species. It's obtained only from the human pituitary, post mortem, and the rate of autopsy is decreasing in our country. In our country, we have only enough growth hormone for maybe half the children who could use it.

I still believe science, particularly biologic science, is for the service of man. This is one of the first hormones I would like to have produced.

Participant: Dr. Yalow, how have changes in radiation safety aspects and knowledge throughout your career, the development of the understanding of the biological effects of radiation and the controls thereof, and perhaps other forms of bureaucracy affected your research as you progressed?

YALOW: First of all, it's relevant that I came from the University of Illinois, where, as you know, the misuse of the cyclotron led to radiation cataracts in one of my schoolmates. I can tell of my own incident. I was sort of a radiation chemist, separating cyclotron targets at the University of Illinois because of my background in chemistry. At that time I had an unexplained illness, with fever and what now might be considered the symptoms of radiation injury.

The university wasn't even equipped to do white counts for an evaluation. I have long been aware of the problem with the potential dangers of radiation. For those of you who heard me on the Marie Curie series,[1] I pointed out that I simply could not understand how, until her death in 1934, she could deny that radiation damage resulted from the careless use of radiation in the laboratories. I'm of the generation that remembers physicians working in fluoroscopy without lead aprons or gloves and dying from leukemia.

I also recognize that we now know a good deal about the dangers of low-level radiation. There must be some middle ground between the foolishness of the early parts of this century and the over-protective ideas of the present. We do have groups of people that we can examine who have had higher than average radiation exposures. Exposure to natural radiation is not constant around the world. There are regions in which people are receiving more than we think are the permissible amounts of radiation for radiation workers and these people seem to have suffered no harm. If we are going to survive, there must be a middle ground. I am very concerned that our fear of radiation is making more people lose lives by not making as effective use as we can of nuclear power sources.

There are many fields in which too much protection may be as lethal as too little protection. We should deal with these better on scientific grounds and less on an emotional basis.

Participant: Among the giants of geology, Dr. Wilson has made a remarkable number of explanations that strike the reader of his short, elegant papers with the thought, "why didn't I think of that?" Could you share with us the thoughts, the processes, that went through your mind when the recognition came of hotspots and the chain of ocean islands that are trailed away from that oceanic hotspot? Were you simply looking at a map one day and this thought popped into your head? Could you share that joy of research with us?

WILSON: All I remember is that it made me very annoyed at the time. I had that idea and it seemed a good one. I don't know how it came to me. As I said, because of extensive travel, because of a background in physics, I tended to look at the earth in a larger scale, and more as a unit, than many geologists did. I remember meeting a geologist who said, "Oh, I couldn't say anything about the geology of Venezuela, I've never worked there." Well, that's ridiculous to my mind. What's the use of geologists writing reports about Venezuela, if other geologists can't read them and can't understand them? It seemed to me that the whole earth should be understandable.

I suppose that's how I saw these chains of islands. After all, they were well known. Betz and Hess had written an account of them.[2] The fact that they get older from one end to the other had been recorded by John Dana, the geologist on the Wilkes expedition [Antarctic, about 1840]. Dana said, "Hawaii, the big island is the youngest. The other islands get older as you go to the west." Hess and Betz said they were along a fault and, therefore, all were of about the same age. So there was already a contradiction and an argument. It didn't seem to me that the current view was the right one, so I made my suggestion and sent it to the *Journal of Geophysical Research*. They turned it down, in the same way that Dr. Yalow experienced. They said my paper had no mathematics in it, no new data, and that it didn't agree with the current views. Therefore, it must be no good. Apparently, whether one gets turned down or not depends largely on the reviewer. The editors, too, if they don't see it your way, or if they think it's something unusual, may turn it down. Well, this annoyed me, and instead of keeping the rejection letter, I threw it in the wastepaper basket. I sent the manuscript to the newly founded *Canadian Journal of Physics*. That was not a very obvious place to send it, but I was a Canadian physicist. I thought they would publish almost anything I wrote, so I sent it there and they published it![3]

Because it was an obscure place to publish a geological article, nobody paid the least attention for several years. If you get a paper turned down, it's because it is either very good or very bad. If it's reasonably good and unusual, then the reviewers may not see that point of view and they may not accept it. If it's bad, they correctly turn it down. You have to guess when you get a paper turned down whether it's a good one or a bad one.

Participant: I'm an amateur explorer of Canadian Arctic islands myself. I was delighted to see adventure sounded as the theme of this session. In this morning's *New York Times* there's a story about a glaciologist, geologist, who is working out every day in a tank in New York in preparation of paddling his kayak around the entire Canadian shield of the North American Continent, something he thinks is going to take him three years.

On the subject of adventure, there's a story that I can tell about the Ontario Science Center in comparison with the Smithsonian. A group of us high-paid Smithsonian executives sat around for several years hoping that it might be possible to replace some of our exhibition hall guards with college students who might take the role of explainers and hosts in the Smithsonian exhibition halls. We were never able to do this, and the Smithsonian exhibit halls are extraordinarily well guarded today, as all of us know. If you go to the Ontario Science Center, there is a cadre of hosts of college students, who are there for short periods of time, to interact with the public and aid in their understanding of the very wonderful things that are on exhibit.

One dimension of adventure is striving to endow our society with the problem-solving capabilities that we need. Perhaps a way toward that is moving our institutions in the fruitful directions that some of our colleagues north of the border have learned.

WILSON: Thank you very much. It's very kind of you to say that. We do, in fact, have security guards as well as students and I have wondered if we could convert them to do something more useful. I can return your compliment. I found one suggestion of what one might do in Disney World, which is a very professional organization. I recently went behind the scenes and toured their operation. They have no director of personnel. They don't employ personnel at Disney World; rather they have a casting director, and all their 12,000 employees are actors! [Laughter]

Participant: I want to ask Dr. Yalow if you felt you could have done as well in any physics-related area as the one you chose. I was impressed by the flexibility of your moving from area to area.

YALOW: I really had the good fortune, as some scientists have had, to be in the right place at the right time. As I tried to convey, I'm a small-science scientist. I like to work without too much money, in a small laboratory, where I can interact very well with a very small group of people.

Unfortunately, the nuclear physics of my generation, the Cavendish-like experiments, where you think of something in the afternoon and you solve it the next day, or that evening, is passing. Experiments in high-energy and particle physics may have twenty-seven names on a paper. They use unbelievable machines and they have to convince somebody to pour in a billion dollars. This isn't for me. I took my radioactivity and moved to another place where I could work on a very small scale. When biomedical investigation becomes a billion-dollar investment, it's not going to be for me anymore. Besides, I knew I wasn't good enough to be a theoretical physicist and do with only paper and pencil.

Participant: I debated which of two questions I wanted to ask you. One seems now to be related. It relates to your career as a woman in science. It strikes me that one of the things that determines whether women are happy and successful in science is how well they get along with their male colleagues. My memory of physics lab is of twenty-seven boys and me. I got out of that. It seems to me what you did was to go into a smaller area where you could establish somewhat more familiar relations.

YALOW: It's a different situation. I was a physicist who went into medicine. I was already kind of a maverick. I was a woman at a time when men were in control in science. Even now I think 98 percent of tenured positions in medical schools are held by men. That ratio is not very much different than in physics. The next generation of women in medicine will of course have higher positions.

I think your approach vis-à-vis men depends upon your own individual security in the matter. I talk about the self-fulfilling prophesy of being disadvantaged and discriminated against. Many people who are discriminated against really agree with those who are doing the discriminating, and develop a certain amount of hostility. They are unable to work in this kind of an atmosphere. I think whenever I was confronted with discrimination, I thought there was something the matter with him, not me. I never really was hostile to him, I just felt sorry for him. [Applause]

EBERT: Thank you very much. Whether the science is small, as in Dr. Yalow's case, or global as in Dr. Wilson's, the ideas have been large. We're very much in their debt.

Chemistry

LINUS PAULING

Research professor, Linus Pauling Institute of Science and Medicine; professor emeritus, Stanford University; director, Institute of Orthomolecular Medicine; member, National Academy of Sciences; winner of the Nobel Prize for Chemistry, 1954, the National Medal of Science, 1974, and the Nobel Peace Prize, 1962, among other honors.

"I have striven for more than sixty years to understand the nature of the world, including living organisms, in terms of their structure. Beginning in 1922, I studied minerals and other inorganic compounds in various ways, then in the 1930's rather simple organic substances, mainly by x-ray diffraction and electron diffraction together with quantum mechanical theory. Then, for a decade or so, I worked on hemoglobin and other proteins, as well as antibodies, which protect us against disease. From 1945 on I was interested in sickle-cell anemia and other hereditary hemolytic anemias as molecular diseases. Since 1954 my main interest has been in mental disease and cancer, especially in relation to orthomolecular prophylaxis and therapeusis. Orthomolecular medicine (which I invented in 1968) is the achievement of the best of health and the prevention and treatment of disease by use of substances normally present in the human body and often required for life, such as the vitamins.

"For many years I was puzzled by the extraordinary specificity of living organisms. I finally became satisfied with my understanding of this specificity while I was working in the field of immunochemistry. The observations that my associates and I made and that other investigators, such as Karl Landsteiner, had made, showed clearly that biological specificity in general depends upon a detailed complementariness in structure of the interacting molecules."

I first talked with Albert Einstein in 1931 in Pasadena. I had seen him five years before in Berlin at a meeting of the Deutschen Physikalischen Gesellschaft (German Physics Society), but I hadn't had an opportunity to talk with him then. In 1931 he came to a seminar that I gave in Pasadena on quantum mechanics and the chemical bond. After the seminar, the reporters asked him what he thought about it. They were always following him around. He said it was "too complicated" for him. In fact, I think that his interest in the details of the world, things that interest a chemist, the difference between one element and another, was not very great. He was interested in what was going on in the understanding of the structure of molecules, but in a rather general way rather than in the detailed way in which I am interested.

After the Second World War, I became a member of the so-called "Einstein Committee," the Emergency Committee of Atomic Scientists, which met every few months in Princeton, and I saw him there. Einstein and I were among the members who felt that the committee should continue to work to educate the people of the United States about the need for controlling nuclear weapons and for preventing war. When the Cold War started, there was enough of a difference of opinion that the committee ceased to exist.

Whenever my wife and I came to Princeton we would go to see him and we always talked for an hour with him in his study on the second floor of his house. I can't remember what we talked about except in a general way. There may have been a little mention, occasionally, of something new in the field of science, but mostly it was about world affairs—about the state of the world, public opinion, and what could be done about it.

What I remember best about him is that it was fun to go there to see him and to talk with him. He would tell jokes, make humorous remarks, and laugh. I remember Einstein laughing heartily with my wife and me at the things brought up in our conversation.

I visited him on Tuesday, the sixteenth of November 1954, a week after I had received notice of having been awarded the Nobel Prize for Chemistry. He made a remark that I wrote down afterwards. He said, "I was glad to see in the *New York Times* that you made good use of the Nobel Prize in your public statement." I had made some statements about the need to get rid of war in the world, and some complaints about the way that Robert Oppenheimer was being treated by the Federal Government.[1] In discussing the nature of the world, he said to us once, "Oxenstjerna [seventeenth-century chancellor of Sweden] said to his son, 'you would be astonished to know with how little wisdom the world is governed.' " This was a point that came up over and over again in our conversations.

Once he made a statement to me that seemed to be a remark of such historical significance that I tried to fix it in my mind. I left soon, and when I was outside his house on Mercer Street I got out my diary and wrote the statement down. He said, "I made one great mistake in my life, when I signed the letter to President Roosevelt recommending that atom bombs be made, but perhaps I may be excused because there was some justification: the danger that the Germans would make them."

I don't know that he really thought that this was a mistake. I think that it is good that there are nuclear weapons in the world because we've been able to avoid the Third World War, which surely would have occurred if these nuclear weapons didn't exist. The great powers would have kept on fighting with one another, sacrificing 20, 40, 60 million people. But, at any rate, he said that. He didn't say, "I made only one great mistake," but I think that I felt the implication that it was only one. I thought how fortunate a man Einstein was, to have made only one great mistake in this world in his life!

I think that he was a fortunate man and a happy man, who enjoyed himself. I've read that when he was fifteen years old he was thinking about the finite value of the speed of light. He asked himself, "what would the world look like if I were riding along, moving at the speed of light?" Of course, ten years later he got essentially the answer to this question: that it is impossible to get up to the speed of light and that no matter how fast you are going the world looks the same. This is a very interesting resolution of the problem. At the same time, he apparently was saying to himself that militarism is wrong. He revolted against militarism and the militaristic attitude prevalent in Germany at that time to such an extent that he succeeded in giving up his German citizenship.

I have enjoyed myself during my whole life. Much of my enjoyment has come from carrying on research. I remember the first seminar that I gave. For a year I did not continue in college, because of not having money. At the Oregon Agricultural College I was given a job, full time, teaching quantitative analysis in 1919 to 1920, and I read the journals. I read the *Journal of the American Chemical Society*, in which, that year, there were several papers by Irving Langmuir on the electronic theory of chemical bonding, based upon G. N. Lewis's 1916 paper,[2] and with this information I gave a seminar on the nature of the chemical bond. It was the first scientific seminar that I had given. I received my degree in chemical engineering in 1922. I had decided to become a chemist in 1913, but I didn't know that there was anything a chemist could do except to be a chemical engineer, so I had studied chemical engineering. I then went to the California Institute of Technology for my graduate work and I was asked to give a seminar, my second seminar. It was on a paper by Einstein, the theory of the speed of sound in a partially dissociated gas. Measurements had been made on a gas, a mixture of nitrogen dioxide and dinitrogen tetroxide, NO_2 and N_2O_4, for which the equilibrium is a function of the pressure. Einstein showed from his development of the theory that you could determine the rates of the forward and reverse reactions by observing the change in the speed of sound as a function of the frequency of the sound. This paper by Einstein shows that he was interested in problems other than just the global problems about special and general relativity and the unified field theory.

When I was a boy eleven or twelve years old I found that I got great satisfaction out of understanding the nature of the world, and there were many questions that I asked. I collected insects and minerals, and read about them. I got reference books out of the library. When I was thirteen, a friend of mine, my own age, showed me some chemical experiments, which entranced me. From that time on I continued to want to understand the properties of substances, to understand, for example, why it is that some substances, are diamagnetic, some are paramagnetic, and some are ferromagnetic. The periodic table of the elements interested me greatly, and I made plots of properties against position in the periodic table.

In the Oregon Agricultural College in my senior year I tried to carry out an experiment that I had formulated on the magnetic properties of iron. It came to nothing. It wasn't too well designed. I didn't know what was known then about the structure of matter and the relations between structure and properties. In 1922 I went to the California Institute of Technology. Arthur Amos Noyes, the head of the Chemistry Department, had suggested that I work on x-ray crystallography with Roscoe Gilkey Dickinson, and this was wonderful. X-ray crystallography had been started by 1913 by the Braggs.[3] Although a moderate number of crystals had been investigated by 1922, there were still thousands more whose structures had not been studied. This was a great opportunity to get information about the interactions of atoms with one another.

I had ideas about which crystals I wanted to know more about. In the first couple of months that I was in Pasadena I synthesized a dozen compounds and grew crystals of them. Dickinson taught me how to investigate them with x rays, but they all turned out to be too complicated to have their structures determined by the methods available at that time. It was a very interesting period because there was no straightforward way of determining the structure of any except the simplest crystals. Dickinson got a crystal of the mineral molybdenite, molybdenum disulfide, for me. I investigated it in the way that he had shown me, and determined its structure. Thus only three months after I had become a graduate student there was something new discovered. We found that the molybdenum atom in this mineral is surrounded by six sulfur atoms at the corners of a trigonal prism. No one had ever seen such a coordination polyhedron before.

I then got interested in how big the atoms are, or the ions in the case of an ionic crystal, such as sodium chloride. A complication is that when you assign sizes to the alkali ions (lithium, sodium, etc.) and the halide ions (fluorine, chlorine, etc.) the ionic radii can be added together to get the observed interionic distance for some of the alkali halide crystals but not for others, the lithium and sodium halides. In these crystals the ions are farther apart than you would expect them to be from the hypothesis of constant ionic radii. I puzzled about that, but it was not until 1928, I think, that the answer was clear to me, although Landé had in fact suggested the answer in 1920.[4]

The answer is that in lithium iodide, where the lithium ion is very small, and the iodide ion is large, the iodide ions are in contact with one another, rather than with the lithium ion. The lithium ion is rattling around in a cavity considerably larger than itself. This result was very satisfying to me when I finally understood it in 1928, not only qualitatively but also quantitatively.

I continued to work on inorganic compounds and, of course, quantum mechanics came along in 1925 and 1926. I'm essentially a theoretical scientist, working on theories. But one sometimes has to go to nature to get the answers to questions, and accordingly I have done experimental work. I determined the structures of scores of minerals, other inorganic compounds, and perhaps one hundred organic compounds by electron diffraction, and I measured the magnetic properties of substances, hemoglobin for example.

By the early thirties I began to wonder about human beings. Before that it had never occurred to me that it might be that science would advance rapidly enough, and be powerful enough, to give us insight into the nature of living organisms. In 1928 A. A. Noyes decided that there should be a Division of the Biological Sciences in the California Institute of Technology.[5] Thomas Hunt Morgan came from Columbia University with a whole crew of geneticists and embryologists to set up the division. I became friendly with them, in particular with a man working in the field of embryology, Albert Tyler.[6] I talked with him a great deal and with Morgan himself.

Morgan was working on specificity in the self-sterility of the sea urchin, and he and Tyler were interested in other examples of biological specificity. Tyler and, later, Karl Landsteiner of the Rockefeller Institute for Medical Research introduced me to the extraordinary phenomenon of biological specificity. For example, if you have a rabbit and you inject a material such as a protein into it, it will produce antibodies that will react with the material. You can extract these antibodies, and you can verify that they will form a precipitate with the protein that was injected into the rabbit, but not with other proteins. This is a very specific reaction. Also, the precipitate redissolves when an excess of the protein is added. There is an analogue in inorganic chemistry. If you take a flask with a solution of silver nitrate in it and start pouring in sodium cyanide, a precipitate of silver cyanide forms. If you then pour in more cyanide, the precipitate redissolves. I understood these reactions. Unipositive silver is bicovalent; it can form two bonds. The cyanide ion is also bicovalent; it has unshared electron pairs at both ends and so it also can form two bonds. Hence these ions form a precipitate that contains very long chains $[Ag\text{---}CN\text{---}Ag\text{---}CN\cdots]$. But if you add an excess of cyanide you get the $[NC\text{---}Ag\text{---}CN]^-$ complex ion, which stays in solution, and accordingly the AgCN precipitate dissolves. This explanation of precipitation and re-solution applies also to the antibody reactions, with the assumption that the antibody molecules are bivalent. My realization that such a complex biological reaction could be understood in chemical terms increased my interest in biology.

In 1936 we (my student Charles Coryell and I) had discovered some striking changes in the magnetic properties of hemoglobin on oxygenation or addition of carbon monoxide. I lectured on this subject when I visited the Rockefeller Institute for Medical Research in New York. Karl Landsteiner, who had discovered the ABO blood groups, the NM blood groups, and the rhesus factor, called me in after my lecture and asked if I could explain some observations that he was making in his laboratory. I didn't know much about the field of serology but during the next year, when I was lecturing in Cornell, he came to Ithaca and spent a week talking to me about it, giving me a short course in the subject. After thinking about the problems for a couple of years, I wrote a paper on the structure of antibodies and the nature of serological reactions.[7] Shortly thereafter, Dan Campbell came to Pasadena as a Rockefeller Fellow and then stayed on as assistant professor of immunochemistry. He, David Pressman, fifteen or twenty students, and some postdoctoral people worked for eight years with me to check up on these ideas. We were able to show that they are right. Biological specificity is based on the interaction of mutually complementary molecules. This is the molecular basis of life.

In 1940 a German physicist, Pascual Jordan, published a paper in the *Zeitschrift für Physik* in which he suggested that there is a special quantum mechanical interaction between two like molecules, and that a gene duplicates itself because of this special quantum mechanical interaction which stabilizes a pair of like molecules in juxtaposition.[8] Max Delbrück[9] asked me, one day in 1940, if I had read that paper. I then read it and talked with him, and then he and I published a paper pointing out that, although this special quantum mechanical interaction exists, it involves energy quantities far smaller than the energy of thermal agitation, and accordingly that it couldn't possibly permit a molecule, such as a gene, to stimulate the production of a replica of itself. Instead, we said that the gene consists of two mutually complementary parts, and that when they separate each of them acts as a template for the synthesis of a replica of the other one. We did not know in 1940 that these two parts are the two chains of DNA in the double helix.

About every ten years I start on another problem. The problems that I work on usually take ten years to solve, and then it seems that the time has come to move on. I shall describe some of these problems.

I have mentioned biological specificity as determined by the detailed molecular complementariness of the interacting molecules. I was astonished when I realized that there is an inorganic example of biological specificity; it is *crystallization*. In a glass of grape jelly, crystals will form of potassium hydrogen tartrate, cream of tartar. If you wash them off and analyze them, they are found to be 99.99 percent pure potassium hydrogen tartrate, separated by the process of crystallization from the thousands of other substances present in the grape jelly. That is really extraordinary specificity, comparable to, although simpler than, the specificity in the production of progeny by living organisms.

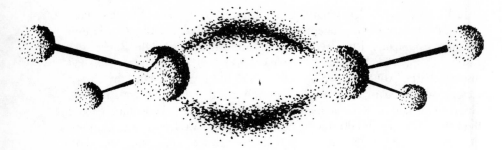

Figure 42. A representation of the ethylene molecule with the double bond shown as two bent single bonds. The four bonds formed by each carbon atom are directed toward the corners of a tetrahedron, with the two tetrahedra sharing an edge in this molecule. [© 1960 by Cornell University]

After 1926 quantum mechanics provided great clarification for chemistry. The tetrahedral arrangement of its bonds, discovered by chemists over a century ago, comes pretty naturally out of the quantum mechanical treatment of the carbon atom. This one idea explains a lot of chemistry. The picture of two tetrahedral carbon atoms sharing an edge requires a molecule such as ethylene, $H_2C = CH_2$, to be planar [fig. 42]. Accordingly, if one replaces two hydrogen atoms on different carbons by chlorine, one can get either the cis isomer, with the chlorine atoms on the same side of the carbon-carbon axis, or the trans isomer. The number of chemical problems that have been solved by application of ideas introduced into science by quantum mechanics is so great that I shall not try to discuss them.

The hydrogen bond came along in 1920. Chemists had found in the last century that acetic acid and other carboxylic acids dissolved in benzene or chloroform have a molecular weight twice as great as was expected for the formulas RCOOH. The reason is that the hydrogens attached to oxygen produce hydrogen bonds holding the two molecules together,

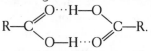

In 1935 I became interested in proteins. Obviously, if you want to understand life you must understand proteins. To show the primitive state of science in those days, in 1939 Karl Niemann and I wrote a paper saying that Irving Langmuir and Dorothy Wrinch were wrong to conclude that insulin and other proteins do not have a polypeptide chain structure, as had been proposed by Emil Fischer around 1900, but have what they called a cyclol structure.[10] We presented several arguments supporting the polypeptide-chain structure, the correctness of which is no longer disputed.

When two amino acids react, a water molecule is lost between the amino group of one and the carboxyl group of the other to form a peptide bond [fig.

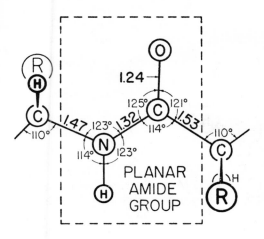

Figure 43. Fundamental dimensions of polypeptide chains as derived from x-ray crystal-structure determinations of amino acids and simple peptides. [© 1960 by Cornell University]

43]. This bond has some double-bond character, as is shown by quantum mechanical considerations and by several observed properties, which require that the six atoms adjacent to the bond lie in one plane. This fact was of great value in the effort to determine how the polypeptide chains of proteins are folded. We knew the dimensions from crystal structure studies of related simple substances [fig. 44], and had the problem of finding the structure of a folded protein, of rotating around these single bonds in such a way that each N-H group would form a hydrogen bond with the oxygen atom of a CO group somewhere along the chain.

We tried to fold the polypeptide chain so as to form these hydrogen bonds, but for some time the solutions eluded us and also other investigators. We worked on this for eleven years. In 1948 one solution was found: it is called the alpha-helix [fig. 44]. The polypeptide chain is folded in such a way as to form N—H···O hydrogen bonds with the CO group of the fourth residue along the chain. The alpha helix is the principal secondary structure of proteins. The first protein structure to have been determined, that of myoglobin, was done by John Kendrew. It contains an iron atom, and it is a rather small protein molecule with molecular weight 16,000 daltons. It has eight sequences of alpha-helix, comprising about 80 percent of the amino-acid residues. Some of the others, about 20 percent, are involved in bending around the corners. Most of the proteins that have been studied by x-ray crystallography turn out to have some alpha-helix sequences in their molecules. Some of them have pleated-sheet structures, with lateral hydrogen bonds. We showed that a pleated-sheet structure is present in silk, both bombyx mori silk and tussah silk. It is also present in many globular proteins whose structures have been determined.

There's a good start being made on understanding enzymatic action in terms of the structure of enzymes. The idea, which is now solidly based, is that the specificity of the enzyme is the result of a detailed complementariness

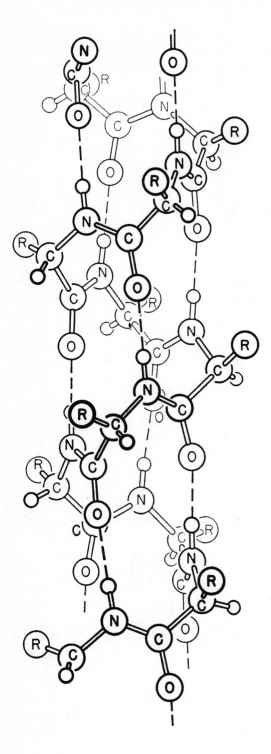

Figure 44. A drawing showing the alpha helix. R represents a side chain: H for glycine, CH₃ for alanine, and
so on for the other eighteen
amino acids commonly
found in proteins. [© 1960
by Cornell University]

in structure of the enzyme to the activated complex, which is an intermediate between the reactant molecules and the products being formed.

With respect to the work on antibodies and antigens, we have the now generally accepted picture of a serological precipitate with bivalent antibody and multivalent antigen, for example, ovalbumin. I assumed in 1940 that the antigen could have as high a valence as its size permitted, getting as many antibody molecules around it as could fit around, but that precipitating antibody was only bivalent. Marrack, an English immunologist, had made the general suggestion of multivalent antibodies, whereas in 1940 I said bivalent because bivalence is enough to do the job. It's sort of an Occam's Razor business.[11] Why should an animal make trivalent antibody if bivalent would give you the serological precipitator that would cause agglutination of cells? We verified bivalence by making compounds, naphthalene derivatives with two benzenearsonic acid groups (R groups) attached. These will give a precipitate with an antibenzenearsonic antiserum. We made a hundred of these compounds with only one benzenearsonic acid haptenic group, and found that none of them would form a precipitate with the antiserum. They blocked the antibody and prevented precipitation with molecules with two or more groups. We analyzed the precipitates and found one molecule with two R groups to each molecule of antibody, 160,000 daltons. Since the molecules with two R groups are bivalent, the antibody must be bivalent. One well-known immunologist said he didn't believe our conclusion. He said that these bifunctional molecules might be only univalent. We then made a substance that requires two rabbits to be allergic to. This substance, RX, consists of one benzenearsonic acid Group R, and one benzoic acid group, X. If we inject an azoprotein with attached X groups into a rabbit, the anti-X antiserum does not participate with this substance. If we inject into another rabbit an azoprotein with R groups attached, the anti-R antiserum also will not precipitate with this substance. But if we mix the two antisera and add the substance RX we get a precipitate, showing that both anti-X and anti-R are involved. On analyzing the precipitate we found one antibody molecule, either anti-X or anti-R, per molecule of this substance, RX. This proved the bivalence of the antibody molecules.

What about complementariness? We made hundreds of derivatives of benzenearsonic acid and of benzoic acid, some substituted in the ortho, meta, or para positions of the benzene rings, and compared them with antibodies against ortho, meta, and para azobenzenearsonic acids. Whenever the substance will fit in, we get strong inhibition of the precipitation with a precipitating antigen. If it doesn't fit, there is less inhibition. Hundreds of these observations, over a period of eight years, led us to the conclusion that the antibodies fit nearly all around the haptenic group to within about a quarter of an atomic diameter. Moreover, we showed that if there is a hydrogen-bond-forming group in the hapten, then there must be a complementary hydrogen-bond-forming group in the antibody. If you replace CO, for example, by CH_2, you get a decrease of about 2.5 kcal/mole in the free energy of combination. We verified also that there is a positive charge in the antibody at about the minimum distance of approach to the negative charge in the haptenic group.

There is no doubt that this detailed molecular complementariness in structure is the basis of life, which is characterized by biological specificity.

I heard about sickle-cell anemia in 1945. When a friend mentioned that the red cells are sickled in the venous blood but regain their normal shape in the arterial blood, I thought at once that this must be a molecular disease, a disease of the hemoglobin molecule. If the patients with this disease had inherited mutated genes such that their hemoglobin molecules had two complementary sticky patches on opposite sides, so that two molecules could juxtapose their complementary regions and stick together, the process would continue, making long chains. These long chains would then line up side-by-side to produce a needlelike crystal that could grow long enough to twist the red cell out of shape, making it sticky because of the change in the red cell membrane, and causing the manifestations of the disease. There is now no doubt that this is the mechanism of the disease. The genetics is clear, too; it is a point mutation that causes the abnormal hemoglobin to be synthesized by the patients. This work was done largely by Dr. Harvey Itano, a young M.D. working with me for a Ph.D. degree. He also discovered hemoglobin C, hemoglobin D, and hemoglobin E, and now there have been about 250 abnormal human hemoglobins discovered—the field of the hemoglobina-pathies has become a big one.

A young man, Emile Zuckerkandl, who had been working at Rostock, in France, came to work with me and stayed for five years.[12] I suggested that he look at the hemoglobins of gorillas and other primates. He made peptide patterns showing the differences in amino acid residues for a number of species. The hemoglobin molecule contains two each of two kinds of polypeptide chains, the alpha chain and the beta chain, each with about 140 amino-acid residues. The human chains differ from those of cow, pig, or horse by about twenty amino-acid residues out of about 140, and from those of Rhesus monkey by about six, but from those of chimpanzee, gorilla, or orangutang by only one. These facts gave us a way to tell when certain evolutionary steps occurred. Horse and human separated 80 million years ago and have twenty amino-acid residues different in their hemoglobin chains, which is 4 million years per evolutionarily effective mutation. For gorilla and human the difference is one amino-acid residue per chain, which gives 4 million years ago as the time when the human species separated from the anthropoid apes, and 24 million years ago when humans and the anthropoids separated from the other primates, the monkeys.

Margoliash and Smith have studied cytochrome molecules.[13] Hemoglobin is a young protein, about 600 million years old. It was evolved from an older protein when it became needed to carry oxygen from lungs to the tissues in large animals. The enzyme cytochrome-C, on the other hand, is about 3 billion years old. It is present in all cells and is needed for oxidation processes. It has about 105 amino-acid residues in the polypeptide chain of its molecules. The number of amino-acid differences in the cytochrome-C chain is six for man and horse, one for man and Rhesus monkey, and none for man and the gorilla. The differences for cytochrome-C are accordingly much smaller than for hemoglobin. The old protein cytochrome-C has not been changing much in the past 50 million, 100 million, or 300 million years.

It is illuminating to compare man and baker's yeast. In sixty of the 105 positions for amino-acid residues of the cytochrome-C chain the same amino acid is found, rather than one of the other nineteen kinds of amino acids. Only in forty-five positions are there differences. This fact shows how closely related we are to baker's yeast, to say nothing of the other organisms with still fewer differences from man. These arguments constituted the start of the field of molecular evolution. The results obtained in this way about the course of evolution of species are pretty much the same as those that the morphological paleontologists, students of evolution based upon morphology, have decided on.

I should, of course, also mention the double helix of Watson and Crick, which is a very nice example of molecular complementariness. The adenine group and the thymine group can form two hydrogen bonds with one another, whereas the guanine group and the cytosine group can form three hydrogen bonds with one another. At each level in the double helix there is a choice between the adenine-thymine pair, the thymine-adenine pair, and the guanine-cytosine pair, and the cytosine-guanine pair, giving complementariness of the two chains, as in the structure that Max Delbrück and I discussed in our 1940 paper, but far more precise and, in fact, to me surprisingly simple. I didn't believe that the complementary structures could be as simple as that, even though in the first edition of my book *The Nature of the Chemical Bond* [1939], I ended the last chapter by mentioning the possible future importance of hydrogen bonds to biology.

In 1953 I decided that I would do something other than study the hereditary hemolytic anemias. I thought that since nobody is working in this new field of molecular diseases, I might as well work on an important disease. What are the important diseases? Cancer and mental illness. But everybody worked on cancer then and nobody worked on mental disease, so I decided to work on mental disease. While thinking about the functioning of the brain I got to thinking about anesthesia. In 1952 I had heard Henry K. Beecher, professor of anesthesiology at Harvard Medical School, give a talk at Massachusetts General Hospital, where I was a member of the Scientific Advisory Board. He said that xenon could produce general anesthesia in humans. This worried me—and this is an illustration of how one makes discoveries. I asked my son, who was a medical student there, what he thought. He didn't have any thoughts about it. I didn't either, and I stayed awake nights before I went to sleep—that is for fifteen minutes perhaps—wondering how it could be that xenon could be an anesthestic agent. Under ordinary conditions, it doesn't interact with anything. I kept worrying about it for a couple of weeks perhaps. I think that I programmed my unconscious mind to continue to think about that problem and to bring it to my conscious mind when something pertinent showed up.

Some years later I read a paper in which someone reported an incorrect structure for chlorine hydrate, one of the crystalline hydrates. I knew that it was wrong. Dick Marsh and I then took x-ray photographs of chlorine hydrate,[14] which had been discovered 150 years before by Michael Faraday, the British chemist and physicist. We determined the correct structure, a very interesting one [Fig. 45], but that wasn't enough for me even though I knew that xenon forms a hydrate. Then one day in 1959 I was opening my mail and I found a manuscript from George Jeffrey in Pittsburgh on the structure of an alkyl ammonium chloride hydrate, an ammonium ion with an alkyl group attached.[15] I thought, this is like the side chain of the amino acid lysine, forming a hydrate like chlorine hydrate or xenon hydrate. I then said to myself, "I understand anesthesia! We have electric oscillations in the brain that constitute consciousness and ephemeral memory. They interact with the material patterns in the brain that constitute permanent memories. The electrically charged side chains of proteins move and help support the electric oscillations. Ions dissolved in the water in the brain move, too. In the presence of the anesthetic agent, it stabilizes the production of one of these hydrates, which immobilizes the charged side chains and the ions. This cuts down the amplitude of the electric oscillations to such an extent that unconsciousness supervenes."

There are twenty water molecules at the corners of a pentagonal dodeca-hedron in the structure that we found for chlorine hydrate. They form hydrogen bonds, tetrahedrally arranged [fig. 45]. The angles are 108°, which is so close to the tetrahedral angle 109° 28' that this is a stable structure, an open structure with a hole in the middle big enough for a xenon molecule, which is a single atom. This crystalline hydrate is stabilized by putting a molecule of chloroform, xenon, or other anesthetic agent in the hole. Thus we have a micro-crystalline hydrate theory of anesthesia. I'm not saying that this is the last word on anesthesia. However, I think that it is a real addition to the original 1899 theory of Meyer and Overton, which is that the anesthetic agent dissolves in the lipid membranes in the brain and changes them in such a way as to produce unconsciousness. A final theory may involve both the lipid phase and the aqueous phase, as well as the membranes in the brain.

A few years ago my associates and I carried out some studies on schizophrenic patients. We gave a standard amount of ascorbic acid, vitamin C, to them by mouth and measured the amount eliminated in the urine

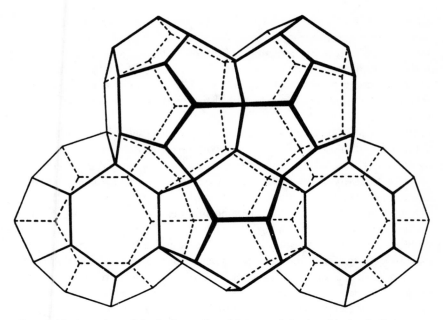

Figure 45. A portion of the hydrogen-bond framework in the chlorine hydrate crystal. The water molecules are grouped into tetrakaidecahedra as well as dodecahedra. Larger molecules and side chains of proteins may occupy the larger polyhedra, and molecules of anesthetic agents such as xenon may occupy the smaller polyhedra also, thus stablilizing the crystalline hydrates. [© 1960 by Cornell University]

during the next six hours. Some other subjects were also studied as controls. The controls eliminated quite a lot, 25 percent of the ingested ascorbate, and most of the schizophrenics eliminated a considerably smaller amount. They are said to have tissue unsaturation, or a special need for this vitamin. Many of the schizophrenic patients were found also to be low excreters of two other vitamins, niacinamide and pyridoxine. We concluded from these observations that a person who is a low excreter in all three of these vitamins, if our results applied to him before he was hospitalized, would have forty times the chance of being hospitalized with acute schizophrenia as one who is not a low excreter in any one of the three.

Recently, we have been working on cancer. It was inevitable that we get around to cancer. The reason is that vitamin C potentiates all of the body's natural protective mechanisms. For example, cancer patients who have a high rate of production of lymphocytes under antigenic stimulation have a good prognosis, whereas those with a low rate have a poor prognosis; and it has been found that a large intake of vitamin C doubles, triples, or even quadruples the rate of production of lymphocytes. In 1971 Dr. Ewan Cameron of Vale of Leven Hospital, Lochlomondaide, Scotland, wrote to ask me how much vitamin C he should try on terminal cancer patients. I answered ten grams per day. He had been trying for years to do something for terminal cancer patients and had written a book about stimulating the body's natural protective mechanisms. He cautiously began treating one terminal cancer patient with vitamin C, and then others, as the patients seemed to respond well. An account of this work is given in the 1979 book *Cancer and Vitamin C* by Dr. Cameron and me.

In figure 46 the times of survival of 100 terminal cancer patients are compared with those of 1,000 matched controls. The 1,000 matched controls die off very fast, and the 100 ascorbate-treated patients die off only one-third as fast, except that a certain percentage of them live much longer. Vitamin C seems to have value for patients with all kinds of cancer.

I now think that there are great possibilities for improving health and controlling disease. I'm not saying that vitamin C and cancer is the only problem that anyone should work on. There are also other things to do, especially controlling militarism and achieving permanent peace in the world.

I am sure that there will always be things for scientists to do. As the physicists learn more and more about the elementary particles (which they no longer call elementary), we begin to think that there may always be some more of these particles, more basic ones, to be discovered; and chemists continue to find interesting problems to work on. In the field of biology, even though I feel pretty well satisfied now with my understanding of the nature of living organisms, I have been surprised by many of the details that have been discovered by the DNA scientists. There are still some things that I don't understand, but I feel convinced that some of them will be understood as the years go by. I continue to hope that I can live a few years longer, and my wife too, another decade, then another decade, and perhaps another decade (chuckles); and enjoy myself by reading about or even participating in the discovery of some new aspects of nature.

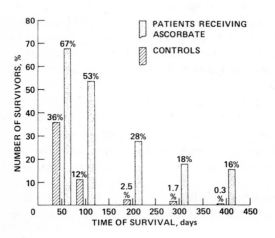

Figure 46. The percentages of the 1,000 controls (matched cancer patients) and the 100 patients treated with ascorbic acid (other treatment identical) who survived by the indicated number of days after being deemed "untreatable." The values at 200, 300, and 400 days for the patients receiving ascorbate are minimum values, corresponding to the date August 10, 1976, when 18 percent of these patients were still alive (none of the controls).

Evolutionary Biology

ERNST MAYR

Professor emeritus of zoology, Harvard University; member, National
Academy of Sciences; former director, Museum of Comparative Zoology,
Harvard; recipient of numerous awards, including the National Medal of
Science, 1970.

"I originally planned to study medicine and did, through the preclinical phase. Then I switched to biology and became an ornithologist; I
have been interested in birds since childhood. Very significant were three
expeditions I led between 1928 and 1930 to New Guinea and the
Solomon Islands, where I observed the importance of geographic variation as an evolutionary process. . . .

"The study of the diversity of nature was rather neglected in evolutionary literature. I pursued this field most actively and made my greatest
contributions to it, promoting the study of evolution in the United States
with the founding of the Society for the Study of Evolution in 1946 and
of the journal *Evolution* in 1947. For twenty years I had the privilege of
working with the finest collection of birds in the world, at the American
Museum of Natural History in New York. I also considered it an honor
and opportunity to be offered the Alexander Agassiz Professorship in
Zoology at Harvard University in 1953."

Let me begin by telling you how I became a scientist. I might say, almost
by accident. I come from a medical family and was born and raised in
Germany. There were physicians in the three generations before me.
Naturally, the family agreed that I should become a doctor. So I studied
medicine and I took my preclinical degree. But while I was a student

Figure 47. A Red-crested Pochard, *Netta rufina*.

something unexpected happened. I was an ardent birdwatcher, and one spring on a small lake near my home town, I observed a pair of Red-crested Pochards [fig. 47]. It was the first time the bird had been observed in central Europe since 1846.

Through this spectacular observation I came to know Professor Erwin Stresemann in Berlin, Germany's leading ornithologist. He persuaded me to work as a volunteer at the Zoological Museum of the University of Berlin during my college vacations. This work so fascinated me that I decided to interrupt my medical career and first get a Ph.D. in biology. What was really in my mind, of course, was to follow in the footsteps of a Humboldt, Darwin, or any of the other great travelers, and explore the wonders of the tropics. Well, I got my Ph.D. in 1926, but then came the seemingly impossible task, to raise the required money for an expedition, in the days before government grants and particularly in a poor country like the Germany of the Weimar Republic.

But luck was with me. At the International Congress of Zoology in Budapest in 1927 I was introduced to Lord Rothschild of Tring, England, the owner of the largest private museum in the world, who was looking for a young zoologist whom he could send to collect birds and other specimens on three rather unexplored mountain ranges of New Guinea. To make a long story short, Lord Rothschild seemed to think I was qualified and half a year later I left Europe for the East Indies. I was tremendously excited, for I was now on my way to New Guinea, which at that time was the least known part of the world except for Greenland, the largest island in the world and the home of a strange and unique flora and fauna, among which the bizarre Birds of Paradise [fig. 48] were particularly remarkable.

Figure 48. Ribbon-tailed Bird of Paradise. [© New York Zoological Society]

Most of you are probably too young to know this, but prior to 1920, it was the height of fashion for a lady to have the plumes of a Bird of Paradise on her hat. Ten thousands of these birds, which occur only in New Guinea, were collected each year by the natives and shipped to the big plume dealers in Paris and London. In addition to the common species, these collections included every once in a while some rare or even new species of Bird of Paradise from some remote mountain range. And this is where Lord Rothschild comes into the picture. He had a standing offer of one hundred pounds (in those days an awful lot of money) for any new species of Bird of Paradise found among the skins collected by the natives. As a result, over the years he was able to describe quite a few of such new species. But this method of collecting was scientifically most unsatisfactory, because one knew nothing about these birds, not even the part of New Guinea from which they might have come. One scientific expedition after another had gone to various parts of New Guinea between 1870 and 1920 to discover the home of these species and to discover new species of other bird families. And they indeed succeeded in discovering the home of most of the so-called "rare Birds of

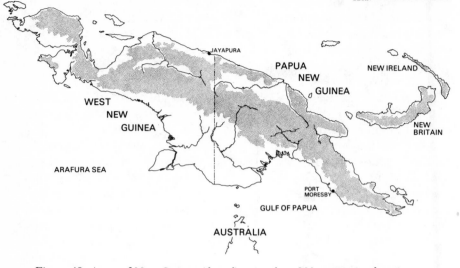

Figure 49. Areas of New Guinea (dotted) more than 200 meters in elevation.

Paradise." But there were about five or six species left which simply could not be rediscovered. What Lord Rothschild wanted me to do was to go to three particular mountain ranges in western New Guinea which so far had been insufficiently explored or not at all.

I would like to tell you all about my trials and tribulations in exploring these untouched and largely uninhabited mountain ranges all alone, except for some native assistants from Java, but my time only permits me to tell you that I obtained a fine collection of birds, mammals, insects, and plants on all three mountain ranges, but saw no hide nor hair of any of Lord Rothschild's rare Birds of Paradise. As far as its principal purpose was concerned, you might say my expedition was a failure. But wait a minute!

My failure to find these birds in some of the last unexplored mountains of New Guinea gave Professor Stresemann in Berlin a bright idea. Maybe there is something fishy about these species; maybe they aren't even good species, he thought. So he examined them very carefully, and was able to prove eventually that each of the so-called species, the home of which could not be found, was actually a hybrid between two other well-known species of Birds of Paradise. You can imagine how pleased I was to have contributed to the solution of this great puzzle of New Guinea ornithology, and to know that my expedition had not been a failure after all. What did I do next?

In the 1920s it was extremely expensive and time-consuming to travel to New Guinea. Consequently, after I had discharged my duties to Lord Rothschild, I stayed in the country, I went to some unexplored mountain ranges in eastern New Guinea, and I finally joined the Whitney South Sea

Expedition of the American Museum of Natural History of New York, which was exploring the islands east of New Guinea with the help of a seventy-two ton schooner. For the next nine months I lived on this schooner and visited many of the Solomon Islands, at that time the least known group of islands in the whole Pacific. Let me remind you that this was 1929–30, long before the Second World War.

What was the particular scientific problem which the Whitney Expedition attempted to solve? It was the problem of the origin of new species, the multiplication of species.

How does this problem of species formation relate to the broader problems of the evolutionary theory? By vastly oversimplifying the story, one can say that there are two great problems of evolution, the origin of adaptation and the origin of the vast diversity of the living world. Natural selection explains how a species can become better and better adapted, but Darwin's opponents never tired of pointing out that natural selection, as such, can never split one species into two. [1] And this problem of how species multiply, one of the two great problems of evolutionary biology, monopolized my interest and my research activities for the next twenty-five years. I am afraid this is a rather technical problem, and it is very difficult to outline in just a few words both the problem and its solution. [2]

But let me try it anyhow. Any one of you who is a bird watcher knows that he can go out in our woods and gardens and find robins, catbirds, Baltimore Orioles, Redstarts, Song Sparrows, and several hundreds of other kinds of birds. But each of these so-called species is well defined and sharply delimited against all others. One will never find an intermediate between two species, except very rarely a more or less sterile hybrid, as in the case of the Birds of Paradise, and such hybrids do not shed any light on the problem of the origin of species. These observations thus confirm that each species is separated from all others by a bridgeless gap. We can now phrase our problem of the origin of species a little more precisely by asking: How is this gap bridged in the origin of a new species? Are there, for instance, perhaps sudden mutations by which a new species may originate by a single jump? As a matter of fact, such a process does occur as a rare event, particularly in plants, by a doubling of the number of chromosomes, but it is not the normal process of speciation, particularly not in the higher animals. How then, do *new* species originate?

This question worried and excited me. I had a feeling that there was something drastically wrong with the whole approach people had chosen. They looked at the species at a particular locality, let us say, the surroundings of Washington, and asked: How do any of these species split into two? But this, I felt, was the wrong question to ask, and I engaged in many heated controversies with my geneticist friends. What then was the right answer to the question of speciation? It was my visit to the Solomon Islands that provided the clues [fig. 50].

This visit made it abundantly clear that speciation is not a problem of

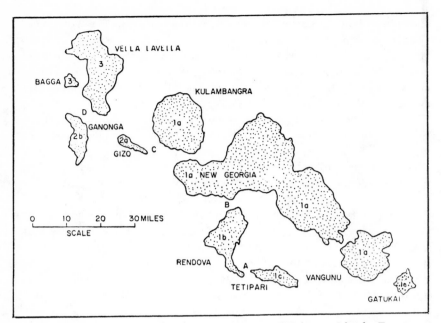

Figure 50. Superspecies Zosterops rendovae in Central Solomon Islands. Extreme localization of related species and subspecies in a tropical archipelago. 1. Rendovae group; 2. luteirostris group; 3. vellalalvella. Groups 1, 2, and 3 are considered full species by some authors, subspecies by others. The subspecies are indicated by lower-case letters. The shortest distances between the islands are A = 1.7 km; B = 2 km; C = 6 km; and D = 5 km. [© 1940 by University of Chicago Press]

individuals, it is a problem of populations. If two populations are separated from each other by a geographical barrier, even though they may have been virtually identical at the beginning, they will eventually become increasingly different as the result of different mutations, different genetic recombinations, and different selection pressures. If this process goes on for long enough a time, let us say hundreds of thousands, or even millions of years, the two daughter populations will eventually be so different that they will behave toward each other as good different species when they come together again. Here, I seemed to have the answer to the problem of speciation and I can hardly describe the pleasure of now knowing the solution to this age-old problem. This process of "geographic speciation" had already been suggested by earlier authors,[3] but was largely ignored by evolutionary geneticists. The usual diagram of the process of species formation is shown in figure 51.

For about twenty years I, along with almost everyone else, was quite happy with this model of so-called geographic speciation. But then I made a number of observations that shook my confidence. I had the feeling that something in my concept of geographic speciation was not quite right. You won't quite

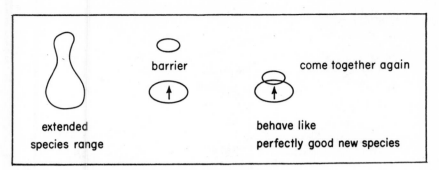

Figure 51. Schematic diagram of the process of species formation.

understand what bothered me, unless I say a few words about the objectives of science.

The lay person often has a rather one-sided concept of scientific advance. He pictures it as a series of discoveries of more or less isolated new facts. He might visualize, as a typical example of a researcher, a paleontologist who goes to a fossil locality and looks for hours and days until he finds a spot where erosion has exposed part of a skeleton or an entire fossil. To be sure, such discovery-making is part of research and I would be the last who would want to minimize the joy and the excitement of the discovery of previously unknown facts or phenomena. I have experienced it many times in my own life. To give you just an example, which I myself had forgotten but which one of my companions on the Whitney Expedition recorded in his diary: "when one day on one of the islands in the Solomons the natives brought a new species and genus of Rails into our camp, I was so elated and excited that I was unable for the rest of the day to skin a bird."[4] The discovery of scientific novelties can be very exciting.

And yet to consider the discovery of an isolated new fact as the whole story of the joys of research would be most misleading. It would give an altogether wrong picture of the nature of science. Science is *not* an accumulation of facts, rather science is the search for an understanding of the world around us.

And such understanding consists in the development of laws, or principles, or concepts, that tie together the accumulated facts and explain their meaning and their causation. I can assure you that the discovery of a new law or a new concept gives an infinitely greater joy than the discovery of an isolated new fact. Like the solution of a difficult puzzle, it gives you great satisfaction.

This brings me back to the problem of geographic speciation. What puzzled me was the relative uniformity of most continental species. Let me illustrate this with the distribution map of a New Guinea Kingfisher. [fig. 52].

Even though the two ends of New Guinea lie in entirely different climatic zones, the birds from the two extremes are virtually indistinguishable. Yet

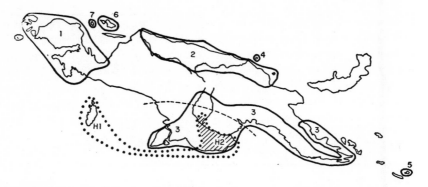

Figure 52. The insular races (4–8) of the New Guinea Kingfisher *Tanysiptera galatea* have developed almost specific rank in their small isolated ranges and are strikingly distinct. The three mainland races (1–3) are very similar to each other and are barely distinguishable. Range expansion of the race number 3 (minor) into south New Guinea has led to an overlap with hydrocharis (H$_1$ and H$_2$), which was formerly isolated by an arm of the sea. [© 1942 by Columbia University Press]

each off-lying island, even if it is only a couple of scores of miles from the New Guinea mainland, is occupied by a local form of kingfishers that is so different that most ornithologists call them different species. How can we explain this? I puzzled over this strange phenomenon for many years until a possible solution suddenly occurred to me one day. All these island populations clearly were founded by single pairs of these rather solitary and nonmigratory birds. These new populations thus showed the so-called founder effect, that is, the founders brought with them only a small fraction of the total variability of the gene pool of the parental mainland population.[5] At first, the founder population will be subject to extreme inbreeding. This, so I postulated, may lead to a drastic reorganization of the gene pool, to a veritable "genetic revolution." With its completely revamped genotype, the new population can start off on an entirely new evolutionary pathway and can become conspicuously different from the parental population.

It was quite a daring theory and after I had published it in 1954,[6] at first no one paid any attention to it. Now, twenty-five years later, it is widely accepted and has been brilliantly confirmed in recent years by the researches of Hampton Carson on the evolution of the Hawaiian *Drosophila* flies.[7] I can assure you that the success of this theory has been the source of great satisfaction and joy for me.

These researches fascinated me, not only for shedding so much light on the previously rather mysterious process of speciation but also because they brought home to me the tremendous importance of biological populations. Populations consisting of uniquely different individuals are one of the major differences between the physical and the biological sciences. While in a population of sodium atoms or hydrogen atoms there are no qualitative differences among these entities, no two individuals are the same in this lecture hall, no two trees are the same in a forest, and no two butterflies are the same on our meadows. The heterogeneity of biological populations and the uniqueness of individuals necessitate for the biologist an entirely different way of thinking than is traditional and appropriate in the physical sciences. As far as the human species is concerned, perceptive people have been long aware of this uniqueness.

No less a person than Albert Einstein himself, I remember, once said in an interview, *"I believe in the uniqueness of the individual."* The importance of this statement cannot be overemphasized. Einstein, of course, thought of the uniqueness of the human individual. Where Einstein's principle of uniqueness is so often violated is by psychologists and educators. That Einstein was able to rise above the conceptual environment of his education as a physicist is just one more piece of evidence for the extraordinary independence of his thinking. But we biologists know that what Einstein so rightly stressed for the human species is equally true for every species of animals and plants. It is the basis of the thinking of every evolutionist from Darwin on, it is the basis of the theory of natural selection,[8] and it is one of the most decisive pieces of evidence for the invalidity of racism, to mention only a few of the applications of the uniqueness-of-every-individual principle. It is *this* principle of the uniqueness of individuals and of populations that is responsible for many of the differences in the thinking of evolutionary biologists and physical scientists. When this had become clear to me, I began to be more and more fascinated with the entire conceptual structure of biology. And this has been my main interest during the past twenty-five years.

The two questions that particularly concern me are: first, what is the conceptual position of biology within the sciences, and secondly, how is biology itself structured conceptually? And I can assure you that trying to answer these questions is puzzle-solving of the most challenging and thrilling kind.

As far as the position of biology is concerned, two extreme viewpoints have been defended for centuries.[9] According to one of them, biological phenomena are exactly the same as those of inanimate objects and can be explained by the laws and principles of the physical sciences. According to the other and extremely different viewpoint, often referred to as vitalism, life is a special force outside the explanatory power of the physical sciences, and it is this special vital power which directs all biological processes.

But is it really true that these are the only two alternatives? I personally say no. With George Gaylord Simpson[10] and other leading biologists, I have concluded that both of the stated explanations are wrong. There is no special life force and no evidence whatsoever to support the claims of the vitalists. Yet, it is equally wrong to say that living organisms are exactly like inanimate objects, because they are not. To be sure, all *processes* in organisms obey the laws of physics and chemistry. But there is a good deal about organisms that is quite different from inanimate objects. What this is, and how the uniqueness of living organisms can be explained in a way that is not in conflict with the laws of physics, is the problem to which I have devoted much of my time and thought in recent decades. This is very exciting research because it touches upon some of man's deepest concerns; it requires preoccupation with some of the oldest problems of western philosophy, from Plato and Aristotle to Hume and Kant. [11]

There is, for instance, the perennial problem of purpose in nature. How can we explain that flowers and bees are so nearly perfectly adapted to each other? How can we explain that the kidney, completely beyond our control, eliminates so efficiently the end products of the protein metabolism of the body? How can we explain the extraordinarily precise goal-directed migrations of migratory birds? Do these phenomena and activities follow definite laws, such as the law of gravity, which makes a heavy object fall, or the first law of thermodynamics, which makes a heated piece of iron in due time assume room temperature? The great philosopher Kant wrote one of his major treatises on this subject, but finally admitted frankly that seeming purposiveness in nature could not be explained by the laws of physics and chemistry. [12] How then is it to be explained? This is the question I asked myself.

When one deals with a conceptually so difficult problem, the worst strategy is to rush in and try to propose a solution. What one needs to do first is to analyze all the terms that have been used in previous arguments, like purpose, goal, law, necessity, etc., and investigate whether these terms may not have several meanings that cause the confusion. This is what I did for the problem of purposiveness in nature, or as it is usually called in philosophy, the problem of teleology. [13] What I discovered was that the term *teleological* had been used as a defining adjective for four entirely different kinds of processes or objects in nature. I cannot go through my entire analysis, and will single out only one of these four categories. For the biologist, the most interesting one is any seemingly goal-directed process, carried out by an individual, such as an annual migration of a migratory bird or the courtship display of a male to a female, or even the development of an individual from the fertilized egg to its perfect adult stage. We now know that in all these cases the end-directed process is controlled by a genetic program, the decoding of which causes the process. Following Pittendrigh, we call such processes *teleonomic* processes in order to distinguish them from other kinds of so-called teleological processes. [14]

The realization that teleonomic processes are governed by genetic programs has deprived them of much of the previously credited mystery. The genetic program in the nucleus of the fertilized egg is like the blueprint of the architect that specifies what the house in the process of being built will look like. The information in what compass direction an individual of a migratory species of birds should migrate is also laid down in the behavior program of that individual; and so is the season when the individual should migrate, and how far. Perhaps you will say, this does not diminish in the slightest the mystery, because how can so much detailed information be coded in the DNA of a single nucleus? In a way you are right. This is indeed a most challenging problem, but not an insoluble one. Molecular biology has been enormously successful in the last twenty years in deciphering ever larger portions of the information encoded in the genetic program. It is indeed awe-inspiring how much information can be laid down in a limited number of molecules, but I insist that, in principle, the problem of teleonomic processes and activities has now been solved.

Enough, let me conclude.

I hope I have been able to show you how exciting the life of a researcher is, and what a satisfaction it is to make discoveries and to find solutions to long-standing problems. But there is more to the life of a scientist than mere puzzle solving. Throughout his research career, again and again, he is up against ultimate questions. Questions concerning meaning, questions concerning the values on which we base our own philosophy of life. Questions that we cannot answer definitively. But the challenge these questions pose makes our life richer and helps us to understand what it means to be a human being.

Thus, research not only brings us abundant joy but it also gives us a deep sense of humility.

Pauling-Mayr Discussion

WILLIAM D. CAREY, Moderator

Executive officer, American Association for the Advancement of Science, and publisher of *Science* magazine; member, Institute of Medicine, National Academy of Sciences; chairman, U.S. side of the bilateral working group on science policy, U.S./USSR Joint Commission on Scientific and Technological Cooperation. Served on a number of White House task forces and Cabinet committees and as assistant director of the U.S. Bureau of the Budget.

Participant: Dr. Pauling, how did you first get interested in the vitamin C question and do you find the evident opposition you're now receiving unprecedented in your career?

PAULING: I'd had problems in getting some of my ideas accepted before vitamin C came along. The concept of resonance in chemistry was misunderstood by some chemists. They raised objections to it on ideological grounds and on scientific grounds, although the scientific grounds were based on a misunderstanding.

I became interested in vitamin C because I decided in 1953 to work on mental illness. I did work, together with several collaborators, on both mental retardation and schizophrenia for ten years, from 1954 to 1964. About that time, I ran across the work of Hoffer and Osmond,[1] the people who discovered that the red oxidation product of epinephrine is psychogenic. It suggested a psychogenetic cause of psychosis, sort of schizophrenialike behavior. They found that giving very large amounts of a vitamin, nicotinic acid or nicotinamide, to persons with schizophrenia, was significantly effective. I also found the work of Stanley Miller when I began reading the literature. Miller had shown in a double blind study that schizophrenic patients benefitted from taking large doses of vitamin C. I was much struck by that, began searching the literature, and found that many other substances, paraminobenzoic acid, glutamic acid, and others affected the functioning of the brain. I wrote a paper, a couple of papers: one—orthomolecular psychiatry—advancing the idea that by changing the concentrations of substances that are normally present in the body, such as vitamins, we may be able to achieve better health, control disease, prevent disease, and even treat disease. That is the way I got started on vitamin C. There's more to the story, but that's the start of it.

Participant: Dr. Pauling, you mentioned that somehow when you want to get a new idea, you instruct your subconscious mind to do it. What trick do you play on your subconscious mind?

PAULING: In general, what I do is sit at a desk and make calculations. If I can't get somewhere by this simple straightforward attack for a while, and if the problem still remains just as much of a problem, a puzzle to me, during the time that I'm doing this, I also think about it at night in bed before going to sleep, sort of as a way to put myself to sleep. If I think about practical problems, the administrative ones that come up in the laboratory— things bother me as an administrator—it just keeps me awake all night. If I think about one of these scientific problems, then I go to sleep. I do this for a couple of weeks, perhaps until I forget to do it anymore. I don't know whether this is right or not, but I've said in the past and continue to say that I think in this way I am impressing the problem on my unconscious with instructions to bring it to the attention of my conscious mind. The instructions are to filter all of the thoughts that go through, all the ideas that come along, and pick out any pertinent one and bring it to my attention.

MAYR: There's a famous story that Darwin was worried about some problem and he had it in the back of his mind for years. Once, when he was riding through the country in a carriage, all of a sudden the illumination came to him.

There's another story among mathematicians that Poincaré, the famous French mathematician, was thinking for weeks and months about a certain problem. One day, when he was trying to catch a trolley car, sort of running up to the trolley and climbing up on the steps, all of a sudden the solution came to him. Whether these stories are apocryphal or not, they show that, once you have a scientific problem that bothers you, it is in your subconscious all the time!

Participant: You talked, Dr. Mayr, about your study of ornithology leading you to postulate the origin of different species in geographically isolated populations. Can this idea be extended to other animal species?

MAYR: As a broad generalization, yes. However, there are indications for the existence of exceptional processes. One species may split into two at a single locality by ecological specialization. Consider insects that are host-specific on particular plants. Most individuals prefer one plant, but a few prefer another plant. Gradually, the two kinds of individuals become two different populations, and eventually, through the selection pressures exerted by their hosts, they may become two different species. This is all still sort of unfinished business, and with only a short time available, I cannot present the open frontiers, which you find in almost any particular problem. However, the business of speciation in birds has been extended to not only other animals but also to plant species. You find this is really the most frequent process by which new species of plants also originate.

Participant: There's a remarkable intersection in the work that both of the speakers have done. Have our explanatory patterns come full circle now with regard to the question of the origins of life? For example, Professor Mayr talked a little bit about teleology and the distinction between the living and the nonliving world. Yet George Wald said that we now know, as was not known in the nineteenth century, that spontaneous generation is a—I think the word he used was a—philosophic necessity.[2] Could either you or both respond?

MAYR: Since this is primarily an evolutionary question, I'll start answering it. Of course, if we believe at all in evolution, there has to be one point in which the gap between nonliving and living was bridged. The interesting thing is that as far as we can tell, this did not happen many times because the genetic code is the same for all organisms and all the molecular pathways that have ever been studied are essentially the same in all organisms. If there had been several different origins of life, one would have to say, at least, that the others have become extinct in the meantime. Only one was the successful one.

   The big problem that I, as a nonbiochemist see, is that proteins have quite a deal of trouble replicating themselves if they aren't being assembled with the help of nucleic acids. On the other hand, nucleic acids don't have much of a function unless they are busy in assembling proteins. I'll toss this thing over to Linus. Does he have any answer to when first proteins and nucleic acids got together and started a partnership?

PAULING: I'll start by answering another question related to this one about the single origin of life. Proteins are made up exclusively of L-amino acid residues, except for glycine, which is not. It is symmetric. One asks, couldn't they just as well be made up of D-amino acid residues? The answer is yes.

However, it is better to make them up entirely of L or entirely of D than of a mixture of D and L, as one can see by looking at protein structure. The pleated sheet is the best example. If you have a pleated sheet made up of L-amino acid residues, all of the residues stick out, way out of the plane of the sheet. There just isn't room for anything but a hydrogen atom in the other position, so they have to be either all L or all D amino acids. The same argument applies to the alpha-helix, but this requires more thought. If these are important secondary structures of proteins, we can understand that we would have either an all L or all D world, so far as amino acids go. The other molecules would also be chiral.

The point now is why are they L rather than D? I think that this means that life started once with L. If it started with D, then D got squeezed out. At any rate, it effectively started once as the L-amino acid world and has continued.

Now consider the other question of just how did life get started with the interaction between amino acids, peptides, and proteins, on the one hand, and the nucleotides and nucleic acids on the other. We can see very easily that in the hot, thin soup, if you have a molecule of nucleic acid, it will catalyze, direct the information of the complementary molecule. That's only the start. As to the rest of the story, I've thought about it some, but I haven't yet written an article about it, so I can't quote myself, and present the whole argument.

Participant: Dr. Mayr, if I understand correctly, the reason you didn't find the six species of the Birds of Paradise is because they were hybrids. Do you just want to talk briefly about hybridization? Do hybrids reproduce? Do you have any specific examples of that? I understand that the Sarus Cranes have come from the Philippines into Australia and have interbred with the Brolga Cranes, creating, some people say, a new species called the Sarolga Crane.

MAYR: Let me be quite dogmatic. Whatever happens if these two species hybridize, it doesn't make a new species because either one will breed back with the two parental species. If this continues, after a while you will simply have one hybrid flock. There are other cases known of such hybrid flocks where, for instance, there are two sparrows in the Mediterranean, the Willow Sparrow, and the ordinary House Sparrow, which in this country we call the English Sparrow. In Spain and in the Balkan Peninsula and in Asia Minor they live happily side-by-side as two good species. For some strange reasons in two places or maybe three places, in Italy, Sardinia, and Algeria, the two kinds of sparrows have hybridized. All the sparrows now found at these localities are hybrids, while at other localities the two parent species continue to coexist. I am uninformed about the Australian Crane story, and have heard nothing about a hybrid species.

Hybridization in plants, if combined with chromosome doubling, can produce new species, but hybridization in diploid species, to the best of my knowledge, will never produce a new species.

Participant: Dr. Pauling, you have said a bit about the granting process. I'd like to ask you for some more comments on it. People talk about how much time is spent on getting grants. You've spoken on how much time is spent on *not* getting grants. Perhaps you can say something about the sociology of this. Perhaps higher-level people, better people should be giving them out.

PAULING: Someone has to make decisions all right. I visited the National Institutes of Health a couple of years ago by invitation and talked with some of the officers about the problem. One suggestion that I made was, and other people have made it too, that a certain fraction of the money available for making grants should be put in a special fund to be given to the support of new ideas that haven't been tested. Here judgment enters as to which ones to support. Someone else who made the same suggestion wrote that, if after five years all of the investigations that had been supported turned out to be successful, it would show that the program wasn't working. You have to have half of them fail if you are really going to be supporting innovative work, new ideas.

I wrote to the National Cancer Advisory Board a year and a half ago that the National Cancer Institute has been doing an excellent job in developmental work, looking at a great many different combinations of anticancer agents; that is, carrying out control clinical trials. However, they don't know how to make discoveries, or how to support workers who will make discoveries, introduce something new in the field, and apparently don't know how to recognize new ideas.

Notes

PAUL FORMAN

1. Translated from the official copy of Einstein's birth certificate, dated March 10, 1915, in the Einstein Archives, Institute for Advanced Study, Princeton. Except where specific references are given, biographical data are derived from the following works: Ronald Clark, *Einstein: The Life and Times* (New York, 1971), which, although never especially sympathetic, is the fullest biography for Einstein's later years but is curiously vague and incomplete on his earlier; Anton Reiser, *Albert Einstein: A Biographical Portrait* (New York, 1930), written by Einstein's son-in-law under a pseudonym, gives the greatest attention to Einstein as a child, but the work, wholly undocumented, contains much that appears to be romantic elaboration of the family's authentic recollections; Philipp Frank, *Einstein: His Life and Times* (New York, 1947), by a theoretical physicist who knew Einstein personally for many years and derived from him some data regarding his childhood; Banesh Hoffman and Helen Dukas, *Albert Einstein: Creator and Rebel* (New York, 1972), is the most readable and best illustrated of the authoritative biographies, written by Einstein's secretary and a physicist who worked with him; Carl Seelig, *Albert Einstein: Ein dokumentarische Biographie* (Zurich, 1954), translated in 1956, and Max Flückiger, *Albert Einstein in Bern* (Berne, 1974), are essentially collections of recollections and extracts of letters, etc.
2. F. Uppenborn, ed., *Die Versorgung von Städten mit elektrischem Strom* (Berlin and Munich, 1891), pp. 61–66, kindly drawn to my attention by Robert Belfield, Smithsonian Fellow, 1978–79.
3. Max Talmey, *The Relativity Theory Simplified and the Formative Period of Its Inventor* (New York, 1932), p. 161.
4. Erik Erikson, paper presented at the Jerusalem Einstein Centennial Symposium, March 16, 1979.
5. Banesh Hoffman, "Einstein and Zionism," in *Proceedings of International Conference on General Relativity and Gravitation*, 7th, Tel-Aviv University, 1974, ed. G. Shaviv and J. Rosen (New York, 1975), pp. 233–42.
6. A. Einstein, "Autobiographical Notes," in *Albert Einstein: Philosopher-Scientist*, ed. P. A. Schilpp (New York, 1951), p. 2.
7. Ibid., p. 4.
8. Ibid.

9. Jagdish Mehra, "Albert Einstein's 'First' Paper," *Science Today* (April 1971): 22–27.

10. Ibid.

11. Roman Jakobson, paper presented at the Jerusalem Einstein Centennial Symposium, March 16, 1979.

12. I am indebted to Lewis Pyenson for information regarding Einstein's secondary schools, the Luitpold Gymnasium, Munich, and the Kantonsschule Aarau, and his performance at the latter school. See Pyenson, "Einstein's Education: Mathematics and the Laws of Nature," *Isis* 71 (1980): 399–425.

13. Translated in Helen Dukas and Banesh Hoffman, eds., *Albert Einstein: The Human Side* (Princeton, N.J., 1979), p. 13.

14. Paul Forman, paper presented at the Jerusalem Einstein Centennial Symposium, March 15, 1979. Also, "Einstein and Newton," *The Wilson Quarterly* (Winter 1979): 102–119.

15. Einstein, "Autobiographische Skizze," in Carl Seelig, ed., *Helle Zeit-Dunkle Zeit: In Memoriam Albert Einstein* (Zurich, 1956), pp. 9–17.

16. Seelig, *Albert Einstein* (1954), p. 35.

17. Max Born, *Die Relativitatstheorie Einstein's* (Berlin, 1920), p. 237.

18. Russell McCormmach, "Einstein, Lorentz, and the Electron Theory," *Historical Studies in the Physical Sciences* 2 (1970): 41–88.

19. Einstein to C. Habicht, May [?], 1905, quoted by Seelig, *Albert Einstein* (1954), p. 89. Although his ideas were not *à la mode*, Einstein had no difficulty publishing them in the premier German physics journal. In the years before the First World War there was no shortage of journal space; indeed, "contributors" usually received honoraria proportionate to the length of their articles, the very reverse of our contemporary "page charges." Compared with some material published by the *Annalen der Physik*, all of Einstein's 1905 papers would have appeared rather solid, and the editor, Wilhelm Wien, probably took them without even consulting his adviser on theoretical physics, Max Planck.

20. Martin J. Klein, "Einstein on Scientific Revolutions," *Vistas in Astronomy* 17 (1975): 113–20.

21. Quoted by Dukas and Hoffman (1979), p. 19.

22. Einstein, "Motive des Forschens," address in celebration of Max Planck's sixtieth birthday, reprinted in *Mein Weltbild*, ed. C. Seelig (Berlin, 1970), pp. 107–10; translated in *Ideas and Opinions* (New York, 1954).

23. Einstein to his sister, Maja, quoted by Dukas and Hoffman (1979), pp. 16–17.

24. Indeed, it has been argued that Einstein did not even know of the Michelson-Morley experiment when he wrote his first papers on the theory of relativity. G. Holton, "Einstein, Michelson, and the 'Crucial' Experiment," *Isis* 60 (1969): 133–97, reprinted in Holton, *Thematic Origins of Scientific Thought* (Cambridge, Mass., 1973).

25. Schilpp, ed., *Einstein: Philosopher-Scientist*, p. 53. Note that the question was not how the world would appear, but how the light wave would appear.

26. Quoted by Seelig (1954), p. 189.

27. Ibid., p. 62.

28. Quoted by Dukas and Hoffman (1979), p. 17.

29. Einstein, prior to 1920, as quoted from memory by Martin Buber, *Knowledge of Man* (New York, 1965), p. 156; *Werke*, vol. 1 (Munich and Heidelberg,

1962), pp. 430–31. Einstein himself spoke of "the promethean element" in the scientific experience in *Festschrift Dr. A. Stodola* (Zurich, 1929), p. 127.

30. *Mein Weltbild* (1970), p. 108.
31. Schilpp, ed., *Einstein: Philosopher-Scientist*, pp. 4–5.
32. Einstein to Mrs. Winteler, June 3, 1897 (Schweizerische Landesbibliothek, Berne).
33. Quoted by Dukas and Hoffman (1979), p. 24.
34. Quoted by Seelig (1954), pp. 183–84.
35. Quoted by Dukas and Hoffman (1979), p. 81.
36. National Museum of American History (formerly History and Technology), Smithsonian Institution, *Einstein: A Centenary Exhibition* (Washington, D.C., 1979), p. 10.
37. Quoted in Hoffman and Dukas (1972), p. 254.
38. Quoted in Seelig, ed., *Helle Zeit-Dunkle Zeit*, p. 50.
39. Einstein, *Out of My Later Years* (New York, 1950), p. 5; from an essay originally published in 1936.

JULIUS AXELROD

1. Peter B. Medawar, *The Art of the Soluble* (London 1967).
2. B. B. Brodie and J. Axelrod, "The Fate of Acetanilide in Man," *Journal of Pharmacology and Experimental Therapeutics* 94 (1948): 29–38.
3. G. Barger and H. Dale, "Chemical Structure and Pharmacological Sympatho-mimetic Action of Amines," *Journal of Physiology* 41 (1910): 19–59.
4. Gordon M. Tomkins, Department of Biochemistry and Biophysics, University of California, San Francisco Medical Center.
5. J. Axelrod, "The Fate of Sympathomimetic Phenylisopropylamines," Ph.D. thesis, George Washington University, 1956.
6. T. R. Elliot, "The Reaction of the Ferret's Bladder to Adrenalin," *Journal of Physiology* 31 (1904): proc. XX; John J. Abel, professor of pharmacology, Johns Hopkins University Medical School.
7. Sir Henry Dale, "Adrenergic Mechanisms," Ciba Foundation Symposium on Adrenergic Mechanisms (London, 1960): 1–5.
8. T. R. Elliot, "The Action of Adrenalin," *Journal of Physiology* 32 (London, 1905): 401–67.
9. Otto Loewi, autobiographic sketch in *Perspectives in Biology and Medicine* 4 (1960):17–18.
10. This is a well-known anecdote. As Friedrich August Kekulé (1829–1896), professor of chemistry at the University of Bonn, tells it:
"I was sitting writing at my textbook, but the work did not progress; my thoughts were elsewhere. I turned my chair to the fire, and dozed. Again the atoms were gamboling before my eyes. This time the smaller groups kept modestly in the background. My mental eye, rendered more acute by repeated visions of this kind, could now distinguish larger structures of manifold conformations; long rows, sometimes more closely fitted together; all twisting and turning in snakelike motion. But look! What was that? One of the snakes had seized hold of its own tail, and the form whirled mockingly before my eyes. As if by a flash of lightening I woke. . . . I spent the rest of the night working out the consequences of the

hypothesis. Let us learn to dream, gentlemen, and then perhaps we shall learn the truth."—August Kekulé, 1865. Morrison and Boyd, *Organic Chemistry* (2d ed., Boston, 1966), p. 313.

11. M. D. Armstrong and A. McMillan, "Identification of a Major Urinary Metabolite of Norepinephrine," *Federation Proceedings* 16 (1957): 146.

12. G. L. Cantoni, "S-Adenosylmethionine: A New Intermediate Formed Enzymatically from L-Methionine and Adenosine-triphosphate, *Journal of Biological Chemistry* 204 (1953): 403–16.

13. J. Axelrod, "O-Methylation of Epinephrine and Other Catechols in Vitro and in Vivo," *Science* 126 (1957): 400–401.

14. L. G. Whitby, J. Axelrod, and H. Weil-Malherbe, "The Fate of H^3-Norepinephrine in Animals," *Journal of Pharmacology and Experimental Therapeutics* 132 (1961): 193–201.

15. G. Hertting, J. Axelrod, I. J. Kopin, and L. G. Whitby, "Lack of Uptake of Catecholamines after Chronic Denervation of Sympathetic Nerves," *Nature* (London) 189 (1961):66.

16. D. E. Wolfe, L. T. Potter, K. C. Richardson, and J. Axelrod, "Localizing Tritiated Norepinephrine in Sympathetic Axons by Electron Microscopic Autoradiography," *Science* 138 (1962):440–42.

17. J. Glowinski and J. Axelrod, "Inhibition of Uptake of Tritiated-Noradrenaline in the Intact Rat Brain by Imipramine and Structurally Related Compounds," *Nature* (London) 204 (1964):1318–319.

18. R. E. Schultes and A. Hofman, *The Botany and Chemistry of Hallucinogens* (Springfield, Mass., 1973), pp. xii and 267.

19. J. Axelrod, "The Enzymatic Formation of Psychotomimetic Metabolites from Normally Occuring Compounds," *Science* 134 (1961):343.

20. D. A. Hamburg, *Psychiatry as a Behavioral Science* (Englewood Cliffs, N.J., 1974), p. 73.

21. A. B. Lerner, J. D. Case, and R. V. Heinzelman, "The Structure of Melatonin," *Journal of the American Chemical Society* 81 (1959): 6084–85.

I. M. SINGER

1. Partly quoted on p. 221 of *Albert Einstein, Creator and Rebel* by Banesh Hoffman and Helen Dukas (New York, 1972).

2. For a brief history of the development of non-Euclidean geometry, see Harold E. Wolfe, *Non-Euclidean Geometry* (New York, 1945).

3. See, for example, M. E. Mayer, "Fibre Bundle Techniques in Gauge Theories," *Lecture Notes in Physics*, vol. 67 (Berlin, Heidelberg, New York, 1977).

AXELROD–SINGER DISCUSSION

1. Located at Bar Harbor, Maine, the Jackson Laboratory specializes in research in mammalian genetics. It was founded 1929.

2. George Monroe Bateman, chemist and educator at Cornell.

3. James Clerk Maxwell (1831–1879), Scottish physicist.

4. See Banesh Hoffman and Helen Dukas, *Albert Einstein, Creator and Rebel* (New York, 1972), p. 50.

5. Marquis de LaPlace; title of Pierre Simon (1749–1827), French mathematician and astronomer.
6. Hendrik Antoon Lorentz (1853–1928), Dutch physicist.
7. Jules Henri Poincairé (1854–1912), French mathematician and physicist.
8. Lord Charles P. Snow, British physicist and author, who has drawn attention to two cultures of science and humanities.
9. See M. E. Mayer, "Fibre Bundle Techniques in Gauge Theories," *Lecture Notes in Physics*, vol. 67 (Berlin, Heidelberg, New York, 1977).
10. Paul Adrien Maurice Dirac (b. 1902), British theoretical physicist and founder of quantum electrodynamics. He attended this lecture. See his paper in *Proceedings of the Royal Society* A133 (1931):60
11. Hoffman and Dukas, p. 190.
12. Robert Olby, *The Path to the Double Helix* (Seattle, 1974).
13. Johannes Kepler, German astronomer, physicist, and mathematician (1571–1630). Derivation may be found in any elementary calculus book.

HOWARD M. TEMIN

1. R. Dulbecco, "Francis Peyton Rous," in *Biographical Memoirs*, vol. 48 (National Academy of Sciences, Washington, D.C., 1976), pp. 275–306.
2. J. D. Watson, *Molecular Biology of the Gene*, 2d. ed. (New York, 1970).
3. A. M. Maxam and W. Gilbert, "A New Method for Sequencing DNA," *Proceedings of the National Academy of Sciences, U.S.A.* (1977):560–65. E. Sanger, G. M. Air, B. G. Barrell, N. L. Brown, A. R. Coulson, J. C. Fiddes, C. A. Hutchison III, P. M. Slocombe, and M. Smith, "Nucleotide Sequence of Bacteriophage of ɸ X174 DNA," *Nature* (London) 265 (1977):687–95. D. Nathans, "Restriction Endonucleases, Simian Virus 40, and the New Genetics," *Science* 206 (1979):903–9.
4. See Temin papers in *Cell* 20 (1980):423–30, and *Nature* (London) 285 (1980):550–54.
5. J. M. Pinney, ed., *Smoking and Health—A Report of the Surgeon General* (U.S. Dept. Health, Education, and Welfare, Washington, D.C., 1979).
6. W. Gilbert, "Why Genes in Pieces?" *Nature* (London) 271 (1978):501

GEORGE B. FIELD

1. A. Einstein, *Annalen der Physik* 17 (1905a):891; English translation in *The Principle of Relativity* (New York, 1923; reprinted by Dover Publications).
2. Ibid., 18 (1905b):639.
3. Ibid., 49 (1916):769.
4. Sir Arthur S. Eddington, *Stars and Atoms* (New Haven, Conn., 1927); *The Nature of the Physical World* (New York, 1931); and *New Pathways in Science* (New York, 1935).
5. H. I. Ewen and E. M. Purcell, "Observation of a Line in the Galactic Radio Spectrum," *Nature* (London) 168 (1951):356.
6. G. B. Field, "An Attempt to Observe Neutral Hydrogen between the Galaxies," *Astrophysical Journal* 129 (1959):525; and "Absorption by Intergalactic Hydrogen", Ibid., 135 (1962):684.

7. G. Herzberg, *Molecular Spectra and Molecular Structure: I. Spectra of Diatomic Molecules* (New York, 1950).
8. A. McKellar, "Molecular Lines from the Lowest States of Diatomic Molecules Composed of Atoms Probably Present in Interstellar Space," *Publications of the Dominion Astrophysical Observatory Victoria* 7 (1949):251.
9. T. Gold and F. Hoyle, *Paris Symposium on Radio Astronomy* (Stanford, Calif., 1959), p. 583.
10. R. Gould and G. Burbidge, "X-rays from the Galactic Center, External Galaxies, and the Intergalactic Medium," *Astrophysical Journal* 138 (1963):969.
11. G. B. Field and R. C. Henry, "Free-Free Emission by Intergalactic Hydrogen," *Astrophysical Journal* 140 (1964):1002.
12. G. B. Field and S. C. Perrenod, "Constraints on a Dense Hot Intergalactic Medium," *Astrophysical Journal* 215 (1977):717.
13. R. A. Alpher and R. Herman, "Evolution of the Universe," *Nature* (London) 162 (1948):774.
14. A. A. Penzias and R. W. Wilson, "A Measurement of Excess Antenna Temperature at 4080 Mc/s," *Astrophysical Journal* 142 (1965):419.
15. R. H. Dicke, P. J. E. Peebles, P. G. Roll, and D. T. Wilkinson, "Cosmic Black-body Radiation," *Astrophysical Journal* 142 (1965):414.
16. C. Arpigny, *Annales d'astrophysique* 27 (1964):393.
17. G. B. Field, G. H. Herbig, and J. L. Hitchcock, "Radiation Temperature of Space at λ 2.6 mm," *Astronomical Journal* 71 (1966):161.
18. G. B. Field and J. L. Hitchcock, *Physical Review Letters* 16 (1966):817; Idem, "The Radiation Temperature of Space at λ 2.6 mm and the Excitation of Interstellar CN," *Astrophysical Journal* 146 (1966c):1.
19. P. Thaddeus, *Annual Review of Astronomy and Astrophysics* 10 (1972):305.
20. R. Thomson and F. W. Dalby, *Canadian Journal of Physics* 46 (1968):2815.
21. D. J. Hegyi, W. A. Traub, and N. P. Carleton, "Cosmic Background Radiation at 1.32 Millimeters," *Astrophysical Journal* 190 (1974):543.
22. D. P. Woody, J. C. Mather, N. S. Nishioka, and P. L. Richards, *Physical Review Letters* 34 (1975):1036.
23. A. Einstein, *Sitzungsberichte der Preussischen Akademie der Wissenschaften* 6 (1917):147; English translation in *The Principle of Relativity*, p. 35.
24. E. Hubble, *Proceedings of the National Academy of Sciences* 15 (1929):168.
25. A. Freidmann, *Zeitschrift für Physik* 10 (1922):377.
26. A. Einstein, *Zeitschrift für Physik* 12 (1931):235.
27. J. H. Taylor, L. A. Fowler, and P. M. McCulloch, "Measurements of General Relativistic Effects in the Binary Pulsar PSR1913 + 16," *Nature* (London) 277 (1979):437.

TEMIN-FIELD DISCUSSION

1. "Birmingham Smallpox Report," *Nature* (London) 277 (1979):75–81.
2. G. Gamow, "Information Transfer in the Living Cell," *Scientific American* 193(4) (1955):70–79.
3. M. Nirenberg, "Genetic Memory," *Journal of the American Medical Association* 206 (1968):1973–77.
4. Fred Sanger, MRC Laboratory of Molecular Biology, Hills Rd., Cambridge,

England; F. Sanger et al., "Nucleotide Sequence of Bacteriophage φX174 DNA," *Nature* (London) 265 (1977):687–95.

5. Derek Bok is a lawyer specializing in labor economics.
6. E. E. David, Jr., "Research Opportunities in Fossil Fuels," *Science* 199 (1978):96.
7. R. A. Manaker and V. Groupé, "Discrete Foci of Altered Chicken Embryo Cell Associated with Rous Sarcoma Virus in Tissue Culture," *Virology* 2 (1956):838–40.
8. Nicholson J. Eastman, *Expectant Motherhood*, 4th ed. rev. (Boston, 1963).
9. W. Gilbert, "Why Genes in Pieces?" *Nature* (London) 271 (1978):501; F. Crick, "Split Genes and RNA Splicing," *Science* 204 (1979):264–71; J. E. Darnell, Jr., "Implications of RNA-RNA Splicing in Evolution of Eukaryotic Cells," *Science* 202 (1978):257–60; J. Rogers, P. Early, C. Carter, K. Calame, M. Bond, L. Hood, and R. Wall, "Two mRNAs with Different 3' Ends Encode Membrane-bound and Secreted Forms of Immunoglobin Chain," *Cell* 20 (1980): 303–12.

WILLIAM SCHUMAN

1. Albert Szent-Györgyi, Hungarian-American biochemist, awarded 1937 Nobel Prize for Physiology or Medicine for work on metabolism with special reference to vitamin C and the catalysis of fumaric acid.
2. "Orpheus with His Lute" (1944)—commissioned by Billy Rose; text by William Shakespeare; G. Schirmer, publisher.

   "The following year (1944) saw, in addition to a film score for an Office of War Information propaganda vehicle called 'Steeltown,' the composition of two works for the producer and director Billy Rose. The first was *Side Show* (the title was later changed to *Circus Overture*), intended to form part of a musical revue entitled 'The Seven Lively Arts.' But Rose changed his thinking about the nature of the revue, and *Side Show* never reached Broadway; shortly thereafter, Schuman rescored the lighthearted piece for full orchestra from its original pit-band instrumentation. Rose also commissioned a musical score for a planned production of Shakespeare's *Henry VIII*, though the project was suspended indefinitely following the unexpected death of the actor selected to play the title role. Schuman had nevertheless completed two numbers, an *a cappella* choral 'Te Deum' (for the play's Coronation Scene) and the exquisite song 'Orpheus with His Lute,' later to inspire two major works." From "William Schuman, A Biographical Essay," by Christopher Rouse, 1980.
3. Concerto for Piano and Orchestra (1942, revised from an unperformed version of 1938)—first performed on January 13, 1943, by Rosalyn Tureck, soloist, and the Saidenberg Sinfonietta, Daniel Saidenberg, conductor. Recorded by GarySteigerwalt, piano; Massachusetts Institute of Technology Orchestra, David Epstein conducting.
4. Pierre Boulez (b. 1925), French composer and conductor, evolved a new synthesis in musical composition by extending serial technique from the realm of pitch to include time relationships and dynamics.
5. Three Colloquies for French Horn and Orchestra: I, Rumination; II, Renewal; III, Remembrance (played without pause), 1979—commissioned by the New York Philharmonic; first performed on January 24, 1980, by Philip F. Myers, soloist, and the New York Philharmonic; Zubin Mehta, conductor.

6. Gunther Schuller, American composer and horn player, known as an active proponent of modern music and jazz.

ROSALYN S. YALOW

1. Ernest Rutherford, British physicist, won the Nobel Prize for Chemistry in 1908 for working out the theory of radioactive disintegration of elements.
2. Jerrold R. Zacharias, professor of physics, Massachusetts Institute of Technology and a member of the National Academy of Sciences.
3. Duane Roller, deceased 1960, first editor of *American Physics Teacher* (now *American Journal of Physics*). Last position; professor of physics, Harvey Mudd College.
4. Robert A. Millikan, Duane Roller, and Ernest C. Watson, *Mechanics, Molecular Physics, Heat and Sound* (Boston, 1937).
5. *Biography of Madame Curie* by Eve Curie (New York, 1937).
6. Rudolf Schoenheimer, deceased 1941, biochemist, College of Physicians and Surgeons.
7. Dr. Bernard Roswit, chief of radiotherapy, Veterans Administration Hospital, Bronx, New York.
8. George Hevesy, Nobel Prize for Chemistry, 1944; *Radioactive Indicators, Their Application in Biochemistry, Animal Physiology and Pathology* (New York, 1948).
9. Dr. Solomon A. Berson, deceased April 1972; Radioisotope Service, Bronx Veterans Administration Hospital; internist 1950–54, chief 1954–68; professor and chairman of medicine, Mt. Sinai School of Medicine, 1968–72.
10. I.A. Mirsky, "The Etiology of Diabetes Mellitus in Man," *Recent Progress in Hormone Research* 7 (1952):437.
11. S.A. Berson, R.S. Yalow, A. Bauman, M.A. Rothschild, and K. Newerly, "Insulin-I^{131} Metabolism in Human Subjects: Demonstration of Insulin Binding Globulin in the Circulation of Insulin-Treated Subjects," *Journal of Clinical Investigation* 35 (1956):170–90.
12. Mirsky, p. 437.

J. TUZO WILSON

1. Ernest Rutherford, New Zealand-born British physicist, won the Nobel Prize for Chemistry in 1908 for working out the theory of radioactive disintegration of elements while at McGill University, Montreal.
2. Professor W. Maurice Ewing (1906–1974), director of Doherty-Lamont Geological Observatory, Columbia University, New York, and Professor Frederick J. Vine, University of East Anglia, United Kingdom. See also *Continents Adrift and Continents Aground*, ed. J. Tuzo Wilson (San Francisco, 1976) and *Continents in Motion* by Walter Sullivan (New York, 1974).
3. Thomas S. Kuhn, *Structure of Scientific Revolutions*, 2d ed. (Chicago, 1970).
4. M. King Hubbert, "Energy Resources of the Earth," *Scientific American*, (September, 1971):69.

YALOW-WILSON DISCUSSION

1. Time-Life five-part series on Marie Curie, shown on Public Broadcasting System beginning Fall 1978 and repeated in 1979. The introduction and concluding remarks for each of the parts were by Dr. Yalow.
2. F. Betz, Jr., and H.H. Hess, "The Flow of the North Pacific Ocean," *Geographic Review* 32 (1942):99.
3. John Tuzo Wilson, "A Possible Origin of the Hawaiian Islands," *Canadian Journal of Physics* 41 (1963):863.

LINUS PAULING

1. J. Robert Oppenheimer (1904–1967), American theoretical physicist, who was accused of being a communist sympathizer by Sen. Joseph R. McCarthy's congressional committee.
2. G.N. Lewis, "The Atom and the Molecule," *Journal of the American Chemical Society* 38 (1916):762.
3. Sir William Henry Bragg and Sir William Laurence Bragg, British physicists, father and son Nobelists, who worked on crystal structure and x-ray spectrometry.
4. A. Landé, *Zeitschrift Physik* 1 (1920):191.
5. A.A. Noyes, chemist and de facto head of California Institute of Technology. Millikan was the front man for the institute, but Noyes most often made the key decisions.
6. Albert Tyler, embryologist, who came to the California Institute of Technology with Thomas Hunt Morgan, the *drosophila* geneticist.
7. "A Theory of the Structure and Process of Formation of Antibodies," *Journal of the American Chemical Society* 62 (1940):2643.
8. Pascual Jordan, "Über quantenmechanische Resonanzanziehung und über das Problem der Immunitätsreaktionen," *Zeitschrift für Physik* 113 (1939):431.
9. Max Delbrück, California Institute of Technology biophysicist, who won the Nobel Prize for Physiology or Medicine in 1968 for work on virology and molecular biology; L. Pauling and M. Delbrück, "The Nature of the Intermolecular Forces Operational in Biological Processes," *Science* 92 (1940):77.
10. "The Structure of Proteins," *Journal of the American Chemical Society* 61 (1939):1860.
11. William of Occam, early-fourteenth-century British philosopher, whose famous postulate was that the most workable solution to a problem is the simplest. There is no necessity to postulate a more complicated solution when the simpler will suffice.
12. Emile Zuckerkandl, president of the Linus Pauling Institute for Science and Medicine, Menlo Park, California.
13. E. Margoliash and E. L. Smith, *Evolving Genes and Proteins*, ed. V. Bryson and H. Vogel (New York, 1965), p. 221.
14. R.E. Marsh, "A Refinement of the Crystal Structure of Glycine," *Acta Crystallogica* 11 (1958):654.
15. M.W. Dougill and G.A. Jeffrey, "The Structure of Dimethyl Oxalate," *Acta Crystallogica* 6 (1953):831.

ERNST MAYR

1. From Jenkin (1867) and Mivart (1871) to De Vries (1901), Bateson (1912), and Goldschmidt (1940).
2. E. Mayr, *Animal Species and Evolution* (Cambridge, Mass., 1963).
3. M. Wagner, K. Jordan, D. S. Jordan, and B. Rensch.
4. W. C. Coultas's diary, on deposit in the library of the Bird Department, American Museum of Natural History, New York.
5. The term "founder effect" was proposed by Mayr in 1942 (*Systematics and the Origin of Species*, p. 237).
6. In *Evolution as a Process*, ed. J. Huxley, A. C. Hardy, and E. B. Ford (London, 1954), pp. 157–80.
7. H. L. Carson and K. Y. Kaneshiro, *Annual Reviews of Ecology and Systematics* 7 (1976):311–45.
8. See chapt. 4 (pp. 95—127) in Th. Dobzhansky et al., *Evolution* (San Francisco, 1977).
9. *Genetics, Paleontology and Evolution*, ed. G. L. Jepsen, G. G. Simpson, and E. Mayr (Princeton, N.J., 1949).
10. Leading American paleontologist, evolutionist, and philosopher, formerly at the American Museum in New York and the Museum of Comparative Zoology at Harvard.
11. Bertrand Russell, *Problems of Philosophy* (Cambridge, 1959).
12. I. Kant, *Kritik der Urteilskraft* (1790); J. D. MacFarland, *Kant's Concept of Teleology* (Edinburgh, 1970).
13. See Mayr, *Evolution and the Diversity of Life* (Cambridge, Mass., 1976), pp. 383–406.
14. C.S. Pittendrigh in *Behavior and Evolution*, ed. A. Roe and C. G. Simpson (New Haven, Conn., 1958).

PAULING-MAYR DISCUSSION

1. M. D. Armstrong and A. McMillan, "Identification of a Major Urinary Metabolite of Norepinephrine," *Federation Proceedings* 16 (1957):146.
2. George Wald, "Radiation and Life," in *Recent Progress in Photobiology*, ed. E. J. Bowen (Blackwell's Scientific Pub., Oxford, 1965), pp. 333–50.

Index

Abel, John J., 29,165
ABO blood groups, 137
Acetanilide, 26, 27
Acetylcholine, 29, 30
Adrenaline, 29, 30, 31
Air, G. M., 167
Alpha helix, 139, 140, 161
Alpher, A., 70, 72, 168
American Astronomical Society, 67, 74
Amphetamine, 28, 30
Anesthesia, 143, 144
Aniline, 26
Annalen der Physik, 127, 128
Antibody, 107
Arecibo Observatory, 77
Arginine, 108
Armstrong, M. D., 166, 172
Arpigny, Claude, 73, 168
Asimov, Isaac, 122
Astronomy, 66, 67, 68, 72, 117
Atiyah, Michael, 38, 44
Atom bomb, 48, 66, 134
Autoradiography, 60
Axelrod, Julius, 25, 39, 45, 47, 48, 52–54,
    57, 165, 166; motivation, 27; reverie,
    30, 34

Baker's yeast, 143
Bankers, 127
Barger, G., 165
Barrell, B. G., 167
Bartels, Johann, 43
Bateman, George Monroe, 49, 166
Bauman, A., 170
Beecher, Henry K., 143
Belfield, Robert, 163
Bell Telephone Laboratories, 70

Berkeley, 72
Berson, Solomon A., 106, 110, 127, 170
Betz, F., Jr., 129, 171
Big-bang cosmology, 67, 70, 72, 74
Biological clock, 35
Biological populations, 154
Biological specificity, 136, 137, 142
Biology, 146, 155
Biomedical investigation, 131
Biophysics, 80
Birds of Paradise, 148–51, 161
Bird watcher, 148, 151
Black holes, 50, 77
Bohr, Niels, 54
Bok, Derek, 82, 169
Boltzmann equation, 70
Bolyai, 42, 43
Bond, M., 169
Born, Max, 164
Boulez, Pierre, 96, 169
Bragg, Sir William Henry, and Sir
    William Laurence, 135, 171
Brain, 32, 34, 88, 122, 144, 159
Brodie, Bernard B., 25, 26, 165
Bromo Seltzer, 26
Brookhaven National Laboratories, 105
Brown, N. L., 167
Bryson, V., 171
Buber, Martin, 164
Burbidge, G., 70, 168
Burke, Bernard, 67

Calame, K., 169
California Institute of Technology, 83,
    134, 135, 136
Cambridge, 44
Cameron, Ewan, 145, 146

Campbell, Dan, 137
Canadian shield, 121
Cancer, 59, 60, 63, 83, 105, 143, 145, 146, 162
Cantoni, G. L., 166
Carcinogens, 28, 63
Carey, William D., 158
Carleton, N. P., 168
Carnegie Institution of Washington, 126
Carson, Hampton L., 154, 172
Carter, C., 169
Case, J. D., 166
Causality, 156
Causation, 153
Cell biology, 126
Central Dogma of Biology, 60
Chemical bond, 134
Chemistry, 133, 134
Chimpanzee, 142
Chromatoelectrophoresis, 109
City College of New York, 26, 104
Clark, Ronald, 163
Clones, 62
Coddington, Earl, 65
Columbia University, 71, 136
Comets, 75
Continental drift, 118, 120, 122
Coordination polyhedron, 135
Copernican revolution, 117
Copernicus, 117, 123
Cornell University, 137
Coryell, Charles, 137
Cosmological constant, 74
Cosmology, 70
Coulson, A. R., 167
Coulta, W. C., 172
Cowell, Henry, 96
Creativity, 41, 53, 54, 81, 86, 88, 98–100, 102
Crick, F., 56, 143, 169
Critics, 94, 95
Crystallization, 137
Curie, Eve, 103, 170
Curie, Marie, 102, 129, 170, 171
Curiosity, 9, 88
Cyanide, 136
Cyanogen, 69, 72, 73
Cyclotron, 128
Cytochrome-C, 142, 143
Cytology, 60

Dalby, F. W., 168
Dale, Sir Henry, 165

Dana, John, 129
Darnell, J. E., Jr., 169
Darwin, 117, 123, 148, 151, 155, 159
David, E. E., 83, 169
Delbrück, Max, 10, 137, 143, 171
Descartes, 34
Diabetics, 107, 113
Diabetologist, 106, 107
Dicke, Robert H., 71, 72, 168
Dickinson, Roscoe Gilkey, 135
Dimethyltryptamine, 33
Dipole, 70; moment, 74
Dirac, Paul Adrien Maurice, 51, 167
Discrimination, 131
DNA, 60, 137, 157; sequencing, 60
Dobzhansky, Th., 172
Doppler effect, 67
Double helix, 137, 143
Double star, 77
Dougill, M. W., 171
Dreams, 29, 40, 165, 166
Dukas, Helen, 163, 164, 166, 167
Dulbecco, R., 167

Early, P., 169
Eastman, Nicholson J., 83, 169
Ebert, James D., 126
Economics, 122, 123, 125, 127
Eddington, Sir Arthur S., 65, 66, 167
Education systems, 52, 53, 55, 96, 124, 125, 155
Einstein, Albert, 13–24, 133, 164, 165, 167, 168; birth, 13; causality, 18; childhood, 13; Swiss citizenship, 17, 134; Committee of Atomic Scientists, 133; fatherland, 24; first academic post, 21; first essay, 16; God, 22, 23, 54; independence, 19, 22; joy, 22, 23, 24; leisure, 23; mistake, 133, 134; de Sitter model, 76; motivation, 22, 24, 40, 50; music, 9, 87; nationality, 16; paradox, 22; physical causation, 16; publication, 128; recognition, 39; religion, 14; research, 13; scientific revolutions, 21; simplicity, 133; student, 19; time, 33; uniqueness, 155; utilitarian ends, 22
Einstein, Hermann, 13, 14
Einstein, Jacob, 13
Einstein, Marie (Maja), 13, 15, 164
Einstein, Pauline Koch, 13, 14
Electron diffraction, 136
Electrophoresis, 108, 109
Elementary particle physics, 51

Elliot, T. R., 29, 165
Embryology, 126, 136
Emergency Committee of Atomic
    Scientists, 133
Emotions, 94
Encephalins, 35
Endocrinology, 114
Endorphins, 35
Engineering, genetic, 62
Epéna, 33, 34
Epinephrine, 159
Erikson, Erik, 163
Euclid, 41
Euclidian geometry, 41, 43, 117
Euclidian space, 51
Evolution, 142, 143, 147, 151, 154, 155,
    160
Evolutionary biology, 147, 151
Evolutionary theory, 151
Ewen, Harold I., 67, 68, 72, 167
Ewing, Maurice W., 120, 170
Expanding universe, 74

Failla, G., 105
Faraday, Michael, 144
Fiddes, J. C., 167
Field George B., 52, 65, 66, 79, 102, 167,
    168; joy, 78
Fischer, Emil, 138
Flückiger, Max, 163
Forman, Paul, 13, 164
Ford, E. B., 172
Founder effect, 154
Fowler, L. A., 168
Frank, Philipp, 163
Franklin Institute in Philadelphia, 59
Franklin, Kenneth, 67
Friedmann, A., 74, 76, 168
Future, 124, 127

GABA, 35
Galaxies, 74
Gamow, George, 67, 80, 81, 168
Gamma-globulin, 107
Gamma rays, 105
Gauge theories, 46, 51
Gauss, 42, 43
Geiger counter, 105
General theory of relativity, 23, 42, 46,
    51, 66, 75, 77
Genes, 63, 84, 137, 154
Genetics, 136, 142

Genetic code, 81, 160
Genetic evolution, 84
Genetic recombinations, 152
Genius, 53, 88
Geographic speciation, 152, 153
Geology, 116–18, 120, 121, 123, 129
Geometry, 42, 45, 55, 117
Geophysics, 117, 119
Georgetown, 82
George Washington University, 29, 67
Gilbert, W., 167, 169
Global geometry, 46, 49, 51
Glowinski, J., 166
God, 22, 23, 54, 117
Gold, T., 70, 168
Goldwater Memorial Hospital, 25, 27
Gorilla, 142, 143
Gould, R., 70, 168
Gravitational fields, 66
Gravity, 46, 66, 76, 297
Gross, Ledwig, 83
Groupé, V., 169
Growth, 123, 124
Growth hormone, 128

Habicht, C., 164
Halide ions, 135
Hallucinogen, 33
Hamburg, David A., 166
Handler, Phil, 81
Haptenic group, 141
Hardy, A. C., 172
Harris, Roy, 86
Harrison, Anna J., 47, 56
Harvard Medical School, 143
Harvard-Monsanto contract, 83
Harvard University, 67, 81, 82, 147
Heeschen, David, 67
Hegyi, D. J., 74, 168
Heinzelman, R. V., 166
Hellegers, André E., 79
Hemoglobin, 136, 137, 142, 143
Henry, Richard C., 70, 168
Herbig, George H., 72, 168
Herman R., 70, 72, 168
Hertting, G., 166
Herzberg, Gerard, 69, 72, 168
Hess, Harry H., 120, 129
Hevesy, George, 105, 106, 170
History, 127
Hitchcock, John L., 72, 168
Hoffer, 159
Hoffman, Banesh, 163, 166, 167

Hofmann, A., 166
Holmes, Arthur, 120
Hood, L., 169
Hoyle, F., 70, 168
Hubbert, M. King, 125, 127, 170
Hubble, E., 168
Humanities, 48, 55
Hunter College, 103, 104, 105
Hutchison, C. A., III, 167
Huxley, J., 172
Hybrid, 150, 161
Hydrogen, 67, 70, 72, 155, 161; bond,
    138, 139, 141, 143
Hyperbolic geometry, 42, 43
Hypothyroidism, 114

Immunology, 52, 109, 126, 136
Institute on Mental Health, 29, 30
Insulin, 106–10, 112–14, 128, 138
"In Sweet Music," 9, 91
Intergalactic space, 67, 68
Integer, 45, 49
Interstellar OH, 72
Iodine-131, 105, 106
ITT Research Laboratories, 105
Itano, Harvey, 142
Ives, Charles, 96

Jackson Laboratory, 83, 166
Jakobson, Roman, 164
Jeans, Sir James, 65
Jeffrey, George A., 144, 171
Jew, 13, 14, 104
Jepson, G. L., 172
Jolles, Susan, 97
Jordan, D. S., 172
Jordan, K., 172
Jordan, Pascual, 137, 171
Jubal Trio, 10
Juilliard School, 86, 88
Jupiter, 67

Kahn, Sue Ann, 95
Kaneshiro, K. Y., 172
Kant, Immanuel, 43, 156, 172
Kekulé, Friedrich August, 30, 165, 166
Kendrew, John, 139
Kepler, Johannes, 56, 167
Kety, Seymour, 30
Klein, Martin J., 164
Kopin, I. J., 166
Kuhn, Thomas S., 122, 170

Landé, A., 171
Landsteiner, Karl, 136, 137
Langley, J. N., 29
Langmuir, Irving, 134, 138
LaPlace, Marquis de, 50, 167
Lebesque integral, 43
Lerner, Aaron B., 34, 166
Lewis, G. N., 134
Lick Observatory, 72
Lincoln Center, 95
Lithium iodide, 136
Lobachevsky, 42, 43
Local geometry, 50
Loewi, Otto, 29, 165
Lorentz, Hendrik Antoon, 51, 167
LSD, 29, 33
Lyman-α photons, 68, 70
Lysine, 108

MacFarland, J. D., 172
Maja, 12, 13, 164
Malthus, 124
Manaker, R. A., 169
Manhattan project, 105
Margoliash, E., 142, 171
Maric, Mileva, 19
Marrack, 141
Marsh, R. E., 171
Massachusetts Institute of Technology, 66
Mathematics, 41, 43, 48, 51, 55, 66, 101,
    102, 124
Mather, J. C., 168
Maxam, A. M., 167
Maxwell, James Clerk, 50, 166; equations,
    22
Mayr, Ernst, 147, 158, 166, 167, 172; joy,
    153, 154, 157; recognition, 154; work,
    150
Marsh, Dick, 144
McArdle Laboratory, 63
McCarthy, Joseph R., 171
McCormmach, Russell, 164
McCulloch, P. M., 168
McInnes, Donald, 9, 90, 92, 94
McKellar, Andrew, 69, 72, 165
McMillan, A., 166
Medawar, Peter B., 27, 165
Mehra, Jagdish, 164
Melatonin, 34, 35
Membranes: structure of, 52
Mental illness, 30, 32, 34, 143
Mercer Street, 67, 133
Mescaline, 33

Methemoglobinemia, 26, 27
Meyer and Overton, 144
Michelson-Morley experiment, 22, 66, 164
Militarism, 134
Milky Way galaxy, 67–69
Millikan, Robert A., 103, 170
Mirsky, Arthur, 106
Mirsky, I. M., 170
Mirsky hypothesis, 113
Molecular biology, 67, 83, 157
Molecular evolution, 143
Molybdenite, 135
Monopole, 51
Morgan, Thomas Hunt, 136, 171
Morphine, 29
Music, 88, 89, 92–98; joy of, 89
Mutations, 151
Myoglobin, 139

N-acetyl para-aminophenol, 27
Nathans, D., 167
National Academy of Sciences, 116, 147
National Cancer Advisory Board, 162
National Cancer Institute, 162
National Institutes of Health, 162
National Heart Institute, 29
National Radio Astronomy Observatory, 67
Natural selection, 151
Neuron, 36
Neurotransmitters, 29–32, 35
Neutron stars, 77
Newerly, K., 170
New Guinea, 119, 147–50, 153
New Guinea Kingfisher, 153, 154
Newton, 50, 56, 66, 75
Niacinamide, 145
Niemann, Karl, 138
Nirenberg, M., 81, 168
Nishioka, N. S., 168
NM blood groups, 137
Nobel Prize, 70, 71, 79, 101, 115, 132, 133
No-growth economy, 123
Non-Euclidean geometry, 41, 42, 46, 166; hyperbolic, 42
Noradrenaline, 30–32, 35, 36
Norepinephrine, 30, 31
Normetanephrine, 30
Noyes, Arthur Amos, 135, 136, 171
Nuclear physics, 67, 103, 131
Nuclear power, 129
Nuclear weapons, 133, 134
Nucleic acid hybridization, 60

Nucleotide sequencing, 61
NYU Medical School, 26

Oak Ridge, 105
Occam's razor, 141
Odell, Noel, 118
Olby, Robert, 167
Ontario Science Centre, 130
Oppenheimer, J. Robert, 133, 171
Orangutang, 147
Oregon Agricultural College, 134, 135
Origin of life, 160
Origin of species, 151, 160
Ornithology, 148, 150, 154, 160
Orthomolecular psychiatry, 159
Osmond, 159
Otis, Herbert, 103
Oxford, 44
Oxytocin, 110

Pancreas, 107
Pasteur, 57
Patent office, 52
Pauling, Linus, 49, 52, 59, 132, 133, 158, 160, 162, 171; joy, 134; motivation, 135; subconcious, 159; unconcious, 144, 159; work, 137, 159
Pedagogy, 125
Peebles, Jim, 72, 168
Peer review, 127, 130
Penzias, Arno A., 70, 71, 72, 73, 168
Peptide bond, 138
Periodic table, 135
Perrenod, S. C., 168
Petroleum, 125, 128
Phi-X 174, 81
Phonetics, 90
Picasso, 100
Pineal gland, 34
Pinney, J. M., 167
Pittendrigh, C. S., 156, 172
Planck, Max, 40, 50, 54, 66, 128, 164
Plate tectonics, 121, 122
Poincairé, Jules Henri, 51, 159
Polycythemia, 105
Population, 152, 154, 155, 160
Postdoctoral fellowship, 54
Potter, L. T., 166
Precambrian geology, 121
Pressman, David, 137
Princeton, 67, 71, 133
Problem solving, 159

Protein, 60, 139.
Prussian Academy of Sciences in Berlin, 21
Psychoactive drugs, 32
Publish-or-perish syndrome, 52
Pulitzer Prize in Music, 86
Pulsar, 77
Purcell, Edward M., 65, 67, 68, 167
Purposiveness, 156
Pyenson, Lewis, 164
Pyridoxine, 145

Quantum field theory, 43, 50
Quantum mechanics, 55, 133, 136–38
Quimby, Edith, 105

Racism, 155
Radar, 66
Radiation, blackbody, 72, 74; gravitational, 76
Radio, 67
Radioactive noradrenaline, 32, 33
Radioactive potassium, 106
Radioactive sodium, 106
Radioimmunoassy, 110–15, 127
Radioisotopes, 105
Radiometric age, 120
Radio telescope, 67, 68
Recombinant DNA, 62, 63, 128
Red-crested Pochards, 148
Regulations, 84
Reiser, Anton, 163
Rejection, 130
Relativity, 39, 46, 55
Rensch, B., 172
Research: accidents of, 55, 70, 102, 147; adventure, 56, 130; advice, 119; career, 54, 85, 131; discovery, 153; failure, 45, 53, 150, 162; frustration, 27, 62; fun, 56, 85, 133; funds, 64; joy, 21–24, 55, 59, 102, 103, 121, 153, 154, 157; luck, 52, 53, 55; money, 47; motivation, 81, 85; opportunities, 64, 125; serendipity, 57; success, 45, 52, 162; thrill, 115
Restriction enzyme mapping, 60
Reverie, 30, 34
Reynolds, Francisco Duran, 83
Rhesus factor, 137
Rhesus monkey, 142, 143
Richards, P. L., 168
Richardson, K. C., 166

Riemann, 42
Rockefeller Institute for Medical Research, 136, 137
Radiation, blackbody, 70
RNA, 60
Roe, A., 172
Rogers, J., 169
Roll, P. G., 72, 168
Roller, Duane, 104, 109, 170
Roswit, Bernard, 170
Rothschild, Lord M. A., 148, 149, 150, 170
Rous sarcoma virus, 59, 60
Rutgers University, 83
Rutherford, Ernest, 102, 118, 170
Russell, Bertrand, 172

Saccheri, Gerolamo, 42, 43
Sanger, E., 167
Sanger, Fred, 81, 168
Schizophrenia, 28, 32, 107, 158, 159
Schizophrenics, 144
Schoenheimer, Rudolph, 170
Schuller, Gunther, 97, 170
Schultes, P. E., 166
Schuman, William, 9, 86, 88, 92; motivation, 90; work, 93, 97, 99
Schwarzschild, Martin, 67
Science opportunities, 64
Scientific discovery, 89
Seelig, Carl, 163, 164
Serology, 137, 141
Shelton, Lucy, 10
Schultes, Richard Evans, 33
Sickle-cell anemia, 142
Simpson, George Gaylord, 155, 172
Singer, I. M., 38, 39, 48, 49, 56, 102; joy, 41; motivation, 39, 44, 45
Singularity, 51
Slocombe, P. M., 167
Smallpox viruses, 80
Smith, E. L., 171
Smithsonian Institution, 59, 81, 130; Radiation Biology Lab, 10
Snow, Lord Charles P., 51, 167
Social sciences, 124
Solomon Islands, 147, 151, 152
Special and general relativity, 134
Speed of light, 77, 134
Speed of sound, 134
Specificity, 139
Spitzer, Lyman, 65, 67

Star ζ Ophiuchi, 72
Star ζ Persei, 72
Stresemann, Erwin, 148, 150
Subconcious, 159
Sullivan, Walter, 170
Swiss Patent Office, 19
Szent-György, Albert, 88, 169

Talmey, Max, 163
Taylor, Frank, 118
Taylor, J. H., 168
Teleology, 156, 160
Temin, Howard M., 58, 59, 80; joy, 62; recognition, 62
Tensor, 66
Thaddeus, P., 168
Theoretical astrophysics, 66
Theoretical biology, 84, 155
Theoretical physicist, 131
Theoretical scientist, 136
Theory: general relativity, 74; gravitation, 67; Meyer and Overton, 144; natural selection, 155; special relativity, 66
Thermodynamics, 104, 155
Thompson, Virgil, 94
Thomson, R., 168
Thyroxine, 114
Toit, du, 120
Tomkins, Gordon M., 28, 165
Topology, 44, 45, 51
Townes, Charles, 71
Traub, W. A., 168
Tylenol®, 27
Tyler, Albert, 136, 171

Ultracentrifugation, 109
Uncertainty principle, 54
Unconscious mind, 144, 159
Unified field theory, 46, 56, 134
University of Illinois, 104, 105, 128
University of Paris, 83
University of Toronto, 121
Uppenborn, F., 163

Vasopressin, 110
Veterans Administration Hospital, Bronx, 83, 101, 105
Vine, Frederick J., 120, 170
Virology, 59, 83
Virola calophylliodea, 33
Vogel, H., 171

Vitalism, 155
Vitamin C, 144–46, 158, 159

Wagner, M., 172
Waika Indians, 34
Wall, R., 169
Watson, Ernest C., 103, 170
Watson, J. D., 80, 167
Watt, James, 122
Wegener, Alfred, 118, 120, 122
Weil-Malherb, H., 166
Weinberg, Steven, 70
Whitby, L. G., 166
Whitney South Sea Expedition, 150, 151, 153
Wien, Wilhelm, 164
Wilkes expedition, 129
Wilkinson, D. T., 72, 168
William of Occam, 171
Wilson, John Tuzo, 116, 117, 126, 129, 170, 171; joy, 117, 124, 129; motivation, 119; recognition, 130; work, 117, 127
Wilson, Robert W., 70, 72, 73, 168
Winteler, Jost, 17, 165
Winteler, Mrs., 165
Wolfe, D. E., 166
Wolfe, Harold E., 166
Woody, D. P., 168
Wrinch, Dorothy, 138

Xenon, 143, 144
X-ray crystallography, 135, 139

Yalow, Rosalyn S., 101, 102, 121, 126, 127, 131, 170; joy, 103; maverick, 131; motivation, 102

Zacharias, Jerrold, 103, 170
Zoological Museum of the University of Berlin, 148
Zuckerkandl, Emile, 142, 171

CREDITS FOR ILLUSTRATIONS

Cover: courtesy of the Archives, California Institute of Technology; figs. 1, 5, 6, 8: Estate of Albert Einstein; figs. 2, 3, 4, 7: ETH, Wiss.-Historische Sammlung; fig. 17: from George Seitz, "Epéna," in *Ethnopharmacologic Search for Psychoactive Drugs, Proceedings of a Symposium Held in San Francisco, California, January 28–30, 1967,* Daniel H. Efron, editor; Bo Holmstedt and Nathan S. Kline, coeditors, Public Health Service Publication no. 1645; fig. 18: from David A. Hamburg, *Psychiatry as a Behavioral Science.* Published by Prentice Hall, Englewood Cliffs, N.J.; fig. 20: adaptation from Julius Axelrod, "Neurotransmitters"; fig. 21: from Jack R. Cooper, Floyd E. Blum, and Robert H. Roth, *The Biochemical Basis of Neuropharmacology.* Reprinted by permission of Oxford University Press; fig. 24: reprinted by permission from *Nature,* vol. 285, pp. 550–54; fig. 29: reproduced from *The Astrophysical Journal,* vol. 215, p. 717; fig. 34: reprinted by permission from *Nature,* vol. 277, p. 437; fig. 35: courtesy of David A. Rothman; figs. 37, 38, 40: reproduced from Rosalyn S. Yalow, "Radioimmunoassay: A Probe for the Fine Structures of Biological Systems," in *Les Prix Nobel en 1977,* Nobel Foundation, 1978, pp. 243–64; fig. 41: from M. King Hubbert, "Energy Resources of the Earth," *Scientific American,* Sept. 1971, p. 69; figs. 42, 43, 44, 45: reprinted from Linus Pauling, *The Nature of the Chemical Bond,* 3d ed. Used by permission of the publisher, Cornell University Press; fig. 46: from Ewen Cameron and Linus Pauling, *Proceedings of the National Academy of Sciences,* vol. 73, pp. 3685–689; fig. 47: courtesy of Dr. Paul A. Johnsgard, Department of Life Sciences, University of Nebraska, Lincoln; fig. 48: courtesy of Dr. Donald Bruning, Curator, Department of Ornithology, New York Zoological Society; fig. 49: courtesy of C. J. Gibbs, National Institutes of Health; fig. 50: reprinted by permission from *The American Naturalist,* vol. 74, pp. 249–78; fig. 52: Ernst Mayr, *Systematics and the Origin of Species,* fig. 15, p. 153. Reprinted by permission of Columbia University Press; Smithsonian photos of I. M. Singer, Anna J. Harrison, James D. Ebert, Linus Pauling, Ernst Mayr, and William D. Carey are by Richard Hofmeister.